THE PRICE

BY **ARTHUR MILLER**

★

★

DRAMATISTS
PLAY SERVICE
INC.

SPECIAL NOTE

THE PRICE was first presented by Robert Whitehead, in association with Robert W. Dowling, at the Morosco Theatre, in New York City, on February 7, 1968. It was directed by Ulu Grosbard, the setting and costumes were by Boris Aronson, and the lighting by Paul Morrison. The cast, in order of appearance, was as follows:

VICTOR FRANZ .... Pat Hingle
ESTHER FRANZ .... Kate Reid
GREGORY SOLOMON .... Harold Gary
WALTER FRANZ .... Arthur Kennedy

PLACE: The Attic Floor of a Manhattan Brownstone

TIME: Today

(In the New York production, the play was performed without an intermission.)

THE PRICE

ACT I

Today.

A dark stage.

Now daylight seeps through a skylight in the ceiling, grayed by the grimy panes. At the same time, light shows through a sooty window at the back which has been X'd out with new whitewash, as in buildings about to be demolished.

The light from above first strikes an overstuffed armchair in center. It has a faded rose slipcover. Beside it on its left, a small table with a filigreed radio of the Twenties on it, on the right a rack with newspapers, behind it a bridge lamp.

The room is progressively seen, and the area around the armchair alone is lived in, with other chairs and a couch relating to it. But outside this area, to the sides and back limits of the room and up the walls is the chaos of ten rooms of furniture squeezed into this one.

There are four couches and three settees strewn at random over the floor, armchairs, wingbacks, a divan, occasional chairs. On the floor and stacked against the three walls up to the ceiling are bureaus; armoires; a tall secretary; a break-front; a long, elaborately carved serving table; end tables; a library table; desks; glass-front bookcases; bow-front glass cabinets; and so forth. Several long, rolled-up rugs and some shorter ones. A windup Victrola, two long sculling oars, bedsteads, trunks. And overhead one large and one smaller crystal chandeliers hang from ropes, not connected to electric wires. Twelve dining room chairs stand in a row along one banked wall.

There is a rich heaviness, something almost Germanic about the furniture, a weight of time upon the bulging fronts and curving chests marshaled against the walls. The room is monstrously crowded and dense, and it is difficult to decide if the stuff is impressive or merely over-heavy and ugly.

An uncovered harp, its gilt chipped, stands alone downstage. Beside it a pail and mop.

At the back, behind a rather makeshift drape long since faded, can be seen a small sink, a hot-plate, and an old icebox.

Up right, a door to the bedroom.

Down left, a door to the corridor and stairway, which are unseen.

We are in the attic of a Manhattan brownstone soon to be torn down.

From the down left door, Patrolman Victor Franz enters in uniform. He halts downstage of dining room table (which is down left). He looks at the room for a moment, then takes upturned chair off table, puts it down right of table, and sits on it and glances at his watch. After a moment he notices hassock is in armchair so he crosses up to it, removes it, and puts it stage left of sofa. In bending over, his left ear pains him. He rubs it. He then crosses to the harp at down right and picks up bucket and mop that are stage left of it. He plucks a string on the harp, then crosses to upstage of armoire and puts mop and bucket on floor.

As he crosses upstage behind the sofa he unbuttons his coat and crosses to down right of armchair, takes cloth cover off of it and looks at the chair for a moment. He then crosses to up left and moves oar from against bookcase to upstage of Walter's chest. He tosses cover on floor up left, sees saber and fencing mask on floor, picks them up. Takes his cap off, puts it on table, takes dust cloth from small statue on furniture upstage of table and dusts inside of mask. He tosses cloth on table and puts mask on. He then turns head from side to side, then crosses to downstage of phonograph with saber.

He takes fencing position, seems about to lunge but doesn't. Removes mask, crosses, hangs it on chair upstage of dining room table. He puts foil on table. He takes another upturned chair from up right corner of table, puts it on floor right of table. He takes off his coat, hangs it on back of this chair. He looks at his wrist watch, then crosses to pile of records, picks one up, lifts lid of phonograph, sees there is a record on. Winds phonograph, starts the turntable, puts needle on. It is Gallagher and Shean singing. He smiles at the corniness. He takes another upturned chair from table and puts it on floor stage right of table between the other two which he had put on floor. He then sits on it. The record ends and he crosses up, lifts needle and places Gallagher and Shean back on the pile. He winds it again and plays the record. It is a laughing record—a woman laughing at a trumpet player. He joins in.

He smiles. Broader. Chuckles. Then really laughs. It gets into him, he laughs more fully. Now he bends over with laughter, taking an unsteady step as helplessness rises in him.

Esther, his wife, enters from the down left door. His back is to her. A half-smile is already on her face as she looks about to see who is laughing with him. She starts toward him.

ESTHER. What in the world is that?

VICTOR. *(Surprised.)* Hi!

> *Lifts the tone arm, smiling, a little embarrassed.*

ESTHER. *(At his L.)* Sounded like a party in here!

> *He gives her a peck.*

(Of the record.) What *is* that?

VICTOR. *(Trying not to openly disapprove.)* Where'd you get a drink?

ESTHER. I told you; I went for my checkup.

> *She laughs with a knowing abandonment of good sense.*

VICTOR. Boy, you and that doctor. I thought he told you not to drink.

ESTHER. *(Crossing R. Laughs.)* I had one!—one doesn't hurt me. Everything's normal anyway. He sent you his best.

> *She looks about.*

VICTOR. Well, that's nice. The dealer's due in a few minutes, if you want to take anything.

ESTHER. *(At U. L. of sofa. Looking around with a sigh.)* Oh dear God—here it is again.

VICTOR. The cleaning woman did a nice job.

> *Closes lid on phonograph.*

ESTHER. *(Crossing U. R. to bedroom, looks in.)* Ya—it never used to be so clean.

> *Closes bedroom door.*

(Indicating the room.) Make you feel funny?

> *Crosses to R. of sofa.*

VICTOR. *(Shrugs.)* No, not really—

ESTHER. *(Shaking her head as she stares about.)* Huh.

> *Puts purse on sofa.*

VICTOR. What.

ESTHER. Time.

VICTOR. I know.

ESTHER. There's something different about it.

VICTOR. No, it's all the way it was. *(Indicating R. side of the room.)* I had my desk on that side and my cot. The rest is the same.

ESTHER. Maybe it's that it always used to seem so pretentious to me and kind of bourgeois. But it does have a certain character…I think some of it's in style again. It's surprising.

VICTOR. Well, you want to take anything?

ESTHER. *(Looking, hesitates.)* I don't know if I want it around. *(Looking around.)* It's all so massive…where would we put any of it?—that chest is lovely.

> *Goes to it, U. R. of sofa.*

VICTOR. That was mine. *(Indicating one across the room.)* The one over there was Walter's. They're a pair.

8

ESTHER. *(Comparing, crossing to U. L. of sofa.)* Oh ya! Did you get hold of him?

> *As though this had been an issue, he rather glances away.*

VICTOR. I called again this morning—he was in consultation.

ESTHER. Was he in the office?

VICTOR. Ya. The nurse went and talked to him for a minute—it doesn't matter. As long as he's notified so I can go ahead.

ESTHER. What about his share?

> *He turns away. She crosses L. to him.*

I don't mean to be a pest, Vic, but there could be some real money here. You're going to raise that with him, aren't you?

VICTOR. I've changed my mind. I don't really feel he owes me anything, I can't put on an act, he's got a right to his half.

> *Esther picks lamp up from U. R. corner of sofa.*

That's probably real porcelain. Maybe it'd go in the bedroom.

> *She puts lamp on table, U. R., then crosses, gets purse from sofa.*

ESTHER. Why don't I meet you somewhere? The whole thing depresses me.

> *Starts L. for door.*

VICTOR. *(Stopping her.)* Why?—it won't take long, relax. *(Taking her to sofa.)* Come on, sit down—the dealer'll be here any minute.

> *Sitting D. end of sofa, Esther puts purse beside her. Victor sits U. of her on sofa.*

ESTHER. There's just something so rotten about it. I'm sorry, I can't help it. There always was. The whole thing's infuriating.

VICTOR. We'll sell it and that'll be the end of it. *(Taking tickets out of shirt pocket.)* I picked up the tickets, by the way.

ESTHER. Oh, good. Boy, I hope it's a good picture.

VICTOR. Better be great, not good. Two-fifty apiece.

> *Puts tickets back in pocket.*

ESTHER. I don't care, I want to go somewhere.—God, what's it all about? When I was coming up the stairs just now, and all the doors

9

hanging open…it doesn't seem possible.

VICTOR. They tear down old buildings every day of the week, kid.

ESTHER. *(Rising, crossing D. of sofa to R. of it.)* I know but it makes you feel a hundred years old.

She goes to the harp.

Well, where's your dealer?

VICTOR. *(Glancing at his watch.)* He's ten minutes late now—he should be here soon.

She angrily plucks the harp.

That should be worth something.

ESTHER. *(Crossing U. a few steps.)* I think a lot of it is. But you're going to have to bargain, you know. You can't just take what they say…

VICTOR. *(Rising, crossing D. of sofa to her. With an edge of protest.)* I can bargain; don't worry, I'm not giving it away.

ESTHER. Because they *expect* to bargain.

VICTOR. Don't get depressed already, will you? We didn't even start.

She crosses L., U. of, sofa and armchair.

I intend to bargain, I know the score with these guys.

She withholds further argument, goes to the phonograph, and firing up some slight gaiety…

ESTHER. What's this record?

VICTOR. *(At R. of sofa.)* It's a Laughing Record. It was a big thing in the Twenties.

ESTHER. *(At D. L. of phonograph. Curiously.)* You remember it?

VICTOR. *(Crossing to L. of U. end of sofa.)* Very vaguely. I was only five or six. Used to play them at parties. You know—see who could keep a straight face—Or maybe they just sat around laughing; I don't know.

ESTHER. That's a wonderful idea!

Their relation is quite balanced, so to speak, he turns to her.

VICTOR. You look good.

She looks at him, an embarrassed smile.

I mean it—

10

ESTHER. *(Crossing to D. L. of armchair.)* I believe you—This is the suit.

VICTOR. *(Crossing to her.)* Oh, is that it! And how much? Turn around.

ESTHER. *(Turning.)* Forty-five, imagine? He said nobody'd buy it, it was too simple.

VICTOR. *(Seizing the agreement.)* Boy, women are dumb; that is really handsome. See, I don't mind if you get something for your money, but half the stuff they sell is such crap... *(Going to her.)* By the way, look at this collar. Isn't this one of the ones you just bought?

> *Esther examines it.*

ESTHER. No, that's an older one.

VICTOR. Well even so. *(Turning up a heel.)* Ought to write to Consumers Union about these heels. Three weeks—look at them!

ESTHER. Well you don't walk straight—You're not going in uniform, I hope.

VICTOR. I could've murdered that guy! I'd just changed, and McGowan was trying to fingerprint some bum and he didn't want to be printed; so he swings out his arm just as I'm going by, right into my container.

ESTHER. *(As though this symbolized.)* Oh, God...

> *Crosses R. to sofa, gets cigarettes and matches from purse.*

VICTOR. I gave it to that quick cleaner, he'll try to have it by six.

ESTHER. Was there cream and sugar in the coffee?

VICTOR. *(Crossing L. a few steps.)* Ya.

ESTHER. He'll never have it by six.

VICTOR. *(Assuagingly.)* He's going to try.

ESTHER. Oh, forget it.

VICTOR. Well it's only a movie...

ESTHER. *(Crossing above hassock to armchair.)* But we go out so rarely—why must everybody know your salary? I want an evening! I want to sit down in a restaurant without some drunken ex-cop coming over to the table to talk about old times.

11

VICTOR. It happened twice. After all these years, Esther, it would seem to me...

ESTHER. *(Sitting armchair.)* I know it's unimportant—but like that man in the museum, he really did—he thought you were the sculptor.

VICTOR. *(Crossing R. to floor lamp which is U. R. of armchair.)* So I'm a sculptor.

> *Lights lamp.*

ESTHER. *(Bridling.)* Well it was nice, that's all! You really do, Vic—you look distinguished in a suit—Why not?

> *She lights cigarette. He crosses R. above sofa, lifts the old radio chassis from floor onto library table.*

I have an idea. Why don't you leave me? Just send me enough for coffee and cigarettes.

VICTOR. See, one drink and look how depressed you get.

ESTHER. Well, it's the kind of depression I enjoy.

VICTOR. *(Applauding by clapping his hands.)* Hot diggety dog, Look, why don't you go off for a couple of weeks with your doctor?

> *She chuckles.*

Seriously. It might change your viewpoint.

ESTHER. I wish I could.

VICTOR. *(Crossing L., sitting U. arm of sofa.)* Well do it. He's got a suit. You could even take the dog—especially the dog.

ESTHER. For God's sake, what have you got against that dog?

VICTOR. Esther, she's a pain in the ass. Eighty dollars in veterinary bills, *(Picking fur off his pants, holding it out to her.)* and every time I put on a uniform it's like a fur coat.

ESTHER. *(Pointing at fur.)* That is not the dog...

VICTOR. So it's the cat. Between the two of them I'm getting up half an hour earlier to brush myself off.

> *She laughs.*

It's not funny. Everytime you go out for one of those walks in the rain I hold my breath what's going to come back with you.

ESTHER. *(Laughing.)* Oh, go on, you love her.

VICTOR. I love her. You get plastered, you bring home strange animals, and I "love" them! I do not love that dog!

> *She laughs with affection, as well as with a certain feminine defiance.*

I don't get the humor; the house stinks.

ESTHER. *(Surprised.)* Well you're not throwing out the cat?!

> *Pause.*

VICTOR. *(Rising, crossing L. to R. of side table by armchair.)* The problem is not the cat, Esther. You're an intelligent, capable woman, and you can't lay around all day. Even something part-time, it would give you a place to go.

ESTHER. I can't go to the same place day after day. I never could and I never will.

> *Rising, crossing L. to dining room table, puts cigarette out in ashtray.*

I'm not quite used to Richard not being there, that's all.

VICTOR. *(Crossing L. to C.)* He's gone, kid. He's a grown man; you've got to do something with yourself.

ESTHER. Did you ask to speak to your brother?

VICTOR. *(Glancing off.)* I asked the nurse. Yes. He couldn't break away.

ESTHER. That son of a bitch. It's sickening.

VICTOR. *(Crossing slowly R. above sofa to R. of it.)* Well what are you going to do? He never had that kind of feeling.

ESTHER. What feeling? To come to the phone after sixteen years? It's common decency.

> *He hits radio chassis as he goes by it.*

(With sudden intimate sympathy.) You're furious, aren't you?

VICTOR. *(Crossing D., sits D. arm of sofa.)* Only at myself. Calling him again and again all week like an idiot... To hell with him, I'll handle it alone and send him his half.

ESTHER. *(Crossing R. to D. R. of hassock.)* But how many Cadillacs can he drive?

VICTOR. That's why he's got Cadillacs.—People who love money don't give it away.

ESTHER. I don't know why you keep putting it like charity. There's such a thing as a moral debt.

VICTOR. You sound like a book sometimes. Moral debt? The guy wouldn't know what I was talking about. Esther, please—

Crosses L. to piano bench, fusses with broken hinge.

—let's not get back on that, will you?

ESTHER. *(Crossing L. to him.)* When are we going to start talking the way people talk!—He could never have finished medical school if you hadn't taken care of Pop.—There could be some real money here.

VICTOR. I doubt that—there are no antiques or—

ESTHER. Just because it's ours why must it be worthless?

VICTOR. Now what's that for?

ESTHER. Because that's the way we think!—We do!

VICTOR. *(Sharply.)* The man won't even come to the phone, how am I going to…?

ESTHER. Then you write him a letter, bang on his door—this *belongs* to you!

VICTOR. *(Seeing how deadly earnest—surprised.)* What are you so excited about?

ESTHER. Well for one thing it might help you make up your mind to take your retirement.

A slight pause.

VICTOR. *(Rather secretively, unwillingly.)* It's not the money been stopping me.

ESTHER. Then what is it?

He is silent.

I just thought that with a little cushion you could take a month or two until something occurs to you that you want to do.

VICTOR. *(Crossing L., looking at wrist watch and out of the door.)* It's all I think about right now, I don't have to quit to think.

14

ESTHER. *(Crossing L. to R. of D. chair, R. of dining room table.)* But nothing seems to come of it.

VICTOR. *(Crossing R., sits on D. side of table.)* Is it that easy? I'm going to be fifty. You don't just start a whole new career. I don't understand why it's so urgent all of a sudden.

ESTHER. *(Laughs.)* All of a sudden! It's all I've been talking about since you became eligible—I've been saying the same thing for three years!

VICTOR. Well it's not three years...

ESTHER. It'll be three years in March! It's *three years*. If you'd gone back to school then, you'd almost have your Masters by now. You might have had a chance to get into something you'd love to do. Isn't that true? *(With total curiosity and sympathy.)* Why can't you make a move?

> *Pause. He is almost ashamed.*

VICTOR. I'll tell you the truth, I'm not sure the whole thing wasn't a little unreal. I'd be fifty-three, fifty-four by the time I could start doing anything.

ESTHER. But you always knew that.

VICTOR. I know, but it's different when you're right on top of it. I'm not sure it makes any sense now.

ESTHER. —But you might have twenty more years, and that's still a long time. Could do a lot of interesting things in that time.

> *Slight pause.*

You're so young, Vic.

VICTOR. I am?

ESTHER. Sure! I'm not, but you are. God, all the girls goggle at you, what do you want?

VICTOR. *(Laughs emptily.)* It's hard to discuss it, Es, because I don't understand it.

ESTHER. Then why don't you write a letter to Walter?

VICTOR. *(Like a repeated story. Crossing R. to C.)* Walter. What's this with Walter again? Every time we start to talk you bring up Walter. You...

ESTHER. He is an important scientist; and that hospital's building a whole new research division. *(Crossing R. to him.)* I saw it in the paper, it's his hospital.

VICTOR. Esther, the man hasn't called me in sixteen years.

ESTHER. But neither have you called him!

> *He looks at her in surprise.*

Well you haven't. That's also a fact.

VICTOR. *(As though the idea were new and incredible.)* What would I call him for?!

ESTHER. Because, he's your brother, he's influential, and he could help—Yes, that's how people do, Vic!—Those articles he wrote had a real idealism, there was a genuine human quality… I mean people do change, you know.

VICTOR. *(Turning away.)* I'm sorry, I don't need Walter.

ESTHER. I'm not saying you have to approve of him; he's a selfish bastard, but he just might be able to put you on the track of something. I don't see the humiliation.

VICTOR. *(Turning to her. Pressed, irritated.)* I don't understand why it's all such an emergency.

ESTHER. Because I don't know where in hell I am, Victor!

> *To her own surprise, she has ended nearly screaming. He is silent. She retracts…*

I'll do anything if I know why, but all these years we've been saying, once we get the pension we're going to start to live…it's like pushing against a door for twenty-five years and suddenly it opens…and we stand there. *(Crossing L., sits D. chair, R. of table.)* —Sometimes I wonder, maybe I misunderstood you, maybe you like the department.

VICTOR. I've hated every minute of it.

ESTHER. I did everything wrong! I swear, I think if I demanded more it would have helped you more.

> *Crossing L. he moves piano bench to R. of her, kisses her cheek, sits on bench.*

VICTOR. That's not true. You've been a terrific wife…

ESTHER. I don't think so. But the security meant so much to you

I tried to fit into that; but I was wrong. God—just before coming here, I looked around at the apartment to see if we could use any of this…and that place is so ugly.

He turns front.

It's worn and shabby and tasteless. And I have good taste! I know I do! It's that everything was always temporary with us. It's like we never were anything, we were always about-to-be. I think back to the war when any idiot was making so much money—that's when you should have quit, and I knew it, I knew it!

VICTOR. *(Turning to her.)* I swear, Es—sometimes you make it sound like we've had no life at all.

ESTHER. God—my mother was so right!—I can never believe what I see. I knew you'd never get out if you didn't during the war— I saw it happening, and I said nothing.—You know what the goddamned trouble is?

He senses the end of her revolt.

VICTOR. What's the goddamned trouble?

ESTHER. We can never keep our minds on money! We worry about it, we talk about it, but we can't seem to *want* it.—I do, but you don't. I really do, Vic. I want it. Vic? *I want money!*

VICTOR. Congratulations.

ESTHER. *(Rising, crossing L. few steps.)* You go to hell!

VICTOR. I wish you'd stop comparing yourself to other people, Esther! That's all you're doing lately.

ESTHER. Well, I can't help it!

VICTOR. *(Rising, puts bench back where it was.)* Then you've got to be a failure, kid, because there's always going to be somebody up ahead of you… Actually, I've even started to fill out the forms a couple of times. *(Crosses L., sits on sofa.)*

ESTHER. *(Crossing R., sits hassock. Alerted.)* What happened?

VICTOR. *(With difficulty—he cannot understand it himself.)* I suppose there's some kind of finality about it that… *(Breaks off.)* It's stupid; I admit it. But you look at that goddamned form and you can't help it—You sign your name to twenty-eight years and you ask yourself—is that all? Is that it? And it is, of course. The

17

trouble is, when I think of starting something new, that number comes up—five-oh—and the steam goes out. The whole thing turns into some kind of joke. *(With a created determination.)* But I'll do something, I will!

Slight pause, he searches for his thought.

I don't know what it is; every time I think about it, it's almost frightening.

ESTHER. I know.

VICTOR. *(Rising, crossing to U. of sofa.)* Like when I walked in here before.

Looks around.

This whole thing…hit me like some kind of craziness. To pile up all this stuff like it was made of gold. I brought up every stick.—I damn near saved the carpet tacks.— *(Crossing L. to U. of armchair.)* I mean you look back, and so many things that seemed so important turn out to be…ridiculous.

He looks at the chair.

Like that whole way I was with him—it's inconceivable to me now.

ESTHER. Well, you loved him.

VICTOR. I know, but it's all words somehow. What was he?—a busted businessman like thousands of others, and I acted like some kind of a mountain crashed. *(Crossing L. to L. of phonograph.)* I don't know—sometimes I wonder maybe I don't sign out because I regret it all more than I realize and I can't face it. Except what's the difference what you do if you don't do the work you love?—It's a luxury, most people never get near it—

Crosses D., sits piano bench. But he loses that reassurance.

I don't know, I tell you there are days when the whole thing is like a story somebody told me. You ever feel that way?

ESTHER. All day, every day.

VICTOR. Oh, come on…

ESTHER. It's the truth.—The first time I walked up those stairs I was nineteen years old. And when you opened that box with your first uniform in it—remember that?—When you put it on the first time?—how we laughed? If anything happened you said you'd call

18

a cop!

They both laugh.

It was like a masquerade. And we were right. That's when we were right.

VICTOR. *(Pained by her pain.)* You know, Esther—every once in a while you try to sound childish and it…

ESTHER. *(Indicating the furniture.)* Please don't talk childishness to me, Victor—not in this room! You let it lay here all these years because you can't have a simple conversation with your own brother,

Esther rises.

and I'm childish?

Vic rises, crosses L. to buffet.

You're still eighteen years old with that man!—I mean I'm stuck, but I admit it!, I can't stand it here. I'm going for a walk.

Crosses R., gets purse from sofa.

VICTOR. OK. Go ahead.

Pause. Esther, saddened, crosses u. gets cigarettes and matches from table r. of armchair, crosses to c.

ESTHER. You got a receipt? I'll get your suit—I just want to get out of here.

Crossing R. to her, Victor gives her receipt.

VICTOR. I don't blame you. It's right off Seventh. The address is on it.

ESTHER. I'm coming back right away.

He crosses R. past her toward radio chassis.

VICTOR. *(Without forgiving himself.)* Do as you please, kid. I can't tell you what to do.

ESTHER. *(Putting receipt in purse.)* You were grinding your teeth again last night, did you know that?

VICTOR. *(Turning at u. l. of sofa.)* Oh, no wonder my ear hurts!

ESTHER. I mean it, it's gruesome; sounds like a lot of rocks coming down a mountain. I wish I had a tape recorder, 'cause if you could hear it, you wouldn't take this self-sufficient attitude.

VICTOR. *(Crossing to R. of her.)* Self-sufficient? I just finished telling you that I...

ESTHER. Then do something! You want to stay on the force then stay on the force, if you don't then don't, and let me know what to do with the rest of my life!

VICTOR. *(Alarmed.)* What's that supposed to mean?

ESTHER. It means jumping out of bed in the morning and wanting to do what you're going to do! You know goddamned well what it means!

> *He is silent, alarmed, hurt. He turns u., crosses to radio chassis. She follows.*

Not that I'm any better.

> *She tries to laugh but he doesn't participate.*

VICTOR. It's okay. I think I get the message.

> *Afraid, she tries to smile.*

ESTHER. Like what?

VICTOR. What other message is there?

ESTHER. What's that?

VICTOR. Oh, one of my old radios that I made. *(Taking large tube out of set.)* Mama Mia, look at that tube.

ESTHER. *(More wonderous than she feels about radios.)* Would that work?

VICTOR. No, you need a storage battery...

> *Recalling, he suddenly looks up at the ceiling.*

ESTHER. *(Looking up.)* What.

VICTOR. One of my batteries exploded, went right through there someplace. *(Points.)* There!—See where the plaster is different?

ESTHER. *(Striving for some spark between them.)* Is this the one you got Tokyo on?

VICTOR. *(Not relenting, his voice dead.)* Ya, this is the monster.

ESTHER. *(With a warmth.)* Why don't you take it?

VICTOR. *(Putting tube back.)* Ah, it's useless.

ESTHER. Didn't you once say you had a lab up here? Or did I dream that?

VICTOR. Sure, I took it apart when Pop and I moved up here. Walter had that wall, *(Pointing to L. wall.)* and I had this. We did some great tricks up here.

> *She is fastened on him. He avoids her eyes and moves waywardly.*

I'll be frank with you, kid—the whole thing is incomprehensible to me. I know all the reasons and all the reasons and all the reasons—and it ends up...nothing.—It's strange, you know?—I forgot all about it—we'd work up here all night sometimes, and it was often full of music. My mother'd play for hours down in the library. *(Crossing D. to harp.)* Which is peculiar, because a harp is so soft. But it penetrates, I guess...

> *Looks at her with an unnameable conflict of feelings.*

ESTHER. You're dear. You are, Vic.

> *He looks at his watch.*

VICTOR. *(Crossing L. toward coat.)* I'll have to call another man. Come on, let's get out of here. *(With a hollow, exhausted attempt at joy.)* We'll get my suit and act rich!

ESTHER. *(Crossing L. to him.)* Vic, I didn't mean that I...

VICTOR. *(Turns R. of table, hugs her.)* Forget it.—Wait, let me put these away before somebody walks off with them.

> *He takes up the foil.*

ESTHER. Can you still do it?

VICTOR. *(His sadness, his distance clinging to him.)* Oh, no—you gotta be in shape for this. It's all in the thighs...

ESTHER. Well let me see, I never saw you do it!

VICTOR. *(Giving the inch. Taking off gun and holster he puts them on table.)* All right, but I can't get down far enough anymore...

ESTHER. Maybe you could take it up again.

VICTOR. *(Taking her to U. of hassock.)* Oh no, it's a lot of work, it's the toughest sport there is. Okay, just stand there.

ESTHER. Me?!

VICTOR. *(Crossing L. to D. of records.)* Don't be afraid. *(Snapping the tip.)* —It's a beautiful foil, see how alive it is? I beat Princeton with this.

> *He laughs tiredly, and makes a tramping lunge from yards away, the button touching her stomach. She springs back as the button touches her.*

ESTHER. God!—Victor!

VICTOR. What!

ESTHER. You looked beautiful.

> *He laughs, surprised and half-embarrassed—when both of them are turned to the door by a loud, sustained coughing out in the corridor. The coughing increases and... Enter Gregory Solomon. In brief, a phenomenon, a man nearly ninety but still straight-backed and the air of his massiveness still with him. He has perfected a way of leaning on his cane without appearing weak. He wears a worn, fur-felt, black fedora, its brim turned down on the right side like Jimmy Walker's—although much dustie—and a shapeless topcoat. His frayed tie has a thick knot, askew under a curled-up collar tab. His vest is wrinkled, his trousers baggy. A large diamond ring is on his left index finger. He is carrying a wrung-out leather briefcase. He hasn't shaved today. Still coughing, catching his breath, trying to brush his cigar ashes off his lapel in a hopeless attempt at business-like decorum, he is nodding at Esther and Victor and has one hand raised in a promise to speak quite soon. Nor has he failed to glance with some suspicion at the foil in Victor's hand.*

VICTOR. *(Crossing L. to U. R. of D. chair.)* Can I get you a glass of water?

> *Solomon gestures an imperious negative, trying to stop coughing.*

ESTHER. *(Crossing L. to U. of piano bench.)* Why don't you sit down?

> *Solomon gestures thanks, sits in the D. chair, D. R. of dining room table, the cough subsiding as he puts briefcase on floor L. of chair.*

You sure you don't want some water?

SOLOMON. *(In a Russian-Yiddish accent.)* Water I don't need; a little blood I could use. Thank you.

He takes deep breaths.

Oh boy. That's some stairs.

ESTHER. You all right now?

SOLOMON. Another couple steps you'll be in heaven. Ah excuse me, officer—I am looking for a party. The name is…

He fingers in his vest.

VICTOR. Franz.

SOLOMON. That's it, Franz.

VICTOR. That's me.

Solomon looks incredulous.

Victor Franz.

SOLOMON. So it's a policeman!

VICTOR. *(Grinning.)* Uh huh.

SOLOMON. What do you know! *(Including Esther.)* You see? There's only one beauty to this lousy business, you meet all kinda people. But I never dealed with a policeman. *(Reaching over to shake hands.)* I'm very happy to meet you. My name is Solomon, Gregory Solomon.

VICTOR. *(Shaking hands.)* This is my wife.

ESTHER. How do you do.

SOLOMON. *(Nodding appreciatively to Esther.)* Very nice.

Takes hat off, puts it on table.

(To Victor.) That's a nice-looking woman.

Extends his hands to her.

How do you do, darling.

They shake hands.

Beautiful suit.

ESTHER. *(Laughs.)* The fact is, I just bought it!

SOLOMON. You got good taste. Congratulations, wear it in good health.

ESTHER. *(Crossing L.)* I'll go to the cleaner, dear. I'll be back soon.

> *Turns L. of Solomon.*

(To Solomon.) Will you be very long?

SOLOMON. With furniture you never know, can be short, can be long, can be medium.

ESTHER. Well you give him a good price now, you hear?

SOLOMON. Ah ha!— *(Waving her out.)* Look you go to the cleaner, and we'll take care everything one hundred percent.

ESTHER. Because there's some very beautiful stuff here...I know it but he doesn't.

SOLOMON. I'm not sixty-two years in the business by taking advantage. Go, enjoy the cleaner.

> *She and Victor laugh.*

ESTHER. *(Shaking her finger at him.)* I hope I'm going to like you, Mr. Solomon.

SOLOMON. Sweetheart, all the girls like me, what can I do?

ESTHER. *(Still smiling—to Victor as she goes to the door.)* You be careful.

> *Victor nods.*

VICTOR. See you later.

> *She goes.*

SOLOMON. I like her, she's suspicious.

VICTOR. *(Laughs in surprise.)* What do you mean by that?

SOLOMON. Well a girl who believes everything how you gonna trust her?

> *Victor laughs appreciatively.*

I had a wife...

> *Breaks off with a wave of the hand.*

Well, what's the difference? Tell me, if you don't mind, how did you get my name?

VICTOR. In the phone book.

SOLOMON. You don't say!—the phone book.

VICTOR. Why?

SOLOMON. *(Cryptically.)* No-no, that's fine, that's fine.

VICTOR. The ad said you're a registered appraiser. *(?)*

SOLOMON. Oh yes. I am registered, I am licensed, I am even vaccinated.

> *Victor laughs.*

Don't laugh, the only thing you can do today without a license is you'll go up the elevator and jump out the window. But I don't have to tell you, you're a policeman, you know this world. *(Hoping for contact.)* I'm right?

VICTOR. *(Reserved.)* I suppose.

SOLOMON. So.

> *He surveys the furniture.*

(With an uncertain smile...) That's a lot of furniture. This is all for sale?

VICTOR. Well, ya.

SOLOMON. Fine, fine. I just like to be sure where we are. *(With a weak attempt at a charming laugh.)* Frankly, in this neighborhood I never expected such a load. It's very surprising.

VICTOR. But I said it was a whole houseful.

SOLOMON. *(With a leaven of unsureness.)* Look, don't worry about it, we'll handle everything very nice.

> *He gets up from the chair and crosses R. below piano bench and turns at L. of hassock.*

I'm not mixing in, Officer, but if you wouldn't mind—what is your connection? How do you come to this?

VICTOR. It was my family.

SOLOMON. You don't say.—Looks like it's standing here a long time, no?

VICTOR. Well, my father moved everything up here after the '29 crash. My uncles took over the house and they let him keep this floor.

SOLOMON. *(As though to emphasize that he believes it.)* I see.

VICTOR. Can you give me an estimate now, or do you have to...?

SOLOMON. *(Crossing R.)* No-no, I'll give you right away, I don't waste a minute, I'm very busy.

> *Lifts cover from D. arm of sofa, mutters, crosses to harp. He plucks a string, listens. Then bends down and runs a hand over the sounding board.*

He passed away, your father?

VICTOR. Oh, long time ago—about sixteen years.

SOLOMON. It's standing here sixteen years?

VICTOR. Well, we never got around to doing anything about it, but they're tearing the building down, so... It was very good stuff, you know—they had quite a little money.

SOLOMON. *(Crossing U. a few steps.)* Very good, yes... I can see. I was also very good; now I'm not so good. Time, you know, is a terrible thing.

> *He is a distance from the harp and indicates it.*

That sounding board is cracked, you know. But don't worry about it, it's still a nice object.

> *Goes to armoire and strokes the veneer.*

It's a funny thing—an armoire like this, thirty years you couldn't give it away; it was a regular measles. Today all of a sudden, they want it again. Go figure it out.

VICTOR. *(Pleased. Putting foil on table and crossing R. to C.)* Well, give me a good price and we'll make a deal.

SOLOMON. Definitely. You see, I don't lie to you—

> *He is pointing U. R. to Victor's chest.*

For instance, a chiffonier like this I wouldn't have to keep it a week.

> *Crosses U. indicating Walter's chest, which is U. L.*

That's a pair, you know.

VICTOR. *(Crossing to bedroom, opens door, then stays D. of door.)* I know. There's more stuff in the bedroom, if you want to look.

SOLOMON. Oh?

> *He goes toward the bedroom.*

What've you got here?

> *He looks into the bedroom, up and down.*

26

I like the bed.

Enters from bedroom, closes door.

That's a very nice carved bed. That I can sell. That's your parents' bed?

VICTOR. Yes. They may have bought that in Europe, if I'm not mistaken. They used to travel a good deal.

SOLOMON. *(Crossing L. above armchair.)* Very handsome, very nice. I like it. Looks a very nice family. That's nice chairs, too. I like the chairs. *(At U. of dining room table.)*

VICTOR. *(Crossing to D. R. of armchair.)* By the way, that dining room table opens up. Probably seat about twelve people.

SOLOMON. *(Looks at the table, crossing to R. of table.)* I know that. Yes. In a pinch even fourteen.

He picks up the foil.

What is this? I thought you were stabbing your wife when I came in.

VICTOR. *(Laughs.)* No, I just found it—I used to fence years ago.

Solomon puts foil back on table.

SOLOMON. You went to college?

VICTOR. For a while, ya.

SOLOMON. That's very interesting.

VICTOR. It's the old story.

SOLOMON. *(Crossing R., sits armchair.)* No, listen—what happens to people is always the main element to me. Because when do they call me? It's either a divorce or somebody died. So it's always a new story. I mean it's the same, but it's different.

VICTOR. You pick up the pieces.

SOLOMON. That's very good, yes. I pick up the pieces. It's a little bit like you, I suppose. You must have some stories, I betcha.

VICTOR. *(Crossing L., gets coat from chair, puts it on.)* Sometimes.

SOLOMON. What are you, a traffic cop, or something…?

VICTOR. No. I'm out in Rockaway most of the time, the airports.

SOLOMON. That's Siberia, no?

VICTOR. *(Laughs.)* I like it better that way.

SOLOMON. You keep your nose clean.

27

VICTOR. *(Smiling.)* That's it. *(Indicating the furniture.)* So what do you say?

SOLOMON. What I say? *(Taking out a cigar.)* You like a cigar?

VICTOR. Thanks, I gave it up a long time ago.

SOLOMON. I can see you are a very factual person.

> *Lights cigar.*

VICTOR. You hit it.

SOLOMON. Couldn't be better. So tell me, you got some kind of paper here? To show ownership?

VICTOR. Well, no, I don't. But... *(Half-laughs.)* I'm the owner, that's all.

SOLOMON. In other words, there's no brothers, no sisters.

VICTOR. I have a brother, yes.

SOLOMON. Ah hah. You're friendly with him. *(?)* —Not that I'm mixing in but I don't have to tell you the average family they love each other like crazy, but the minute the parents die is all of a sudden a question who is going to get what and in five minutes you're covered with cats and dogs...

VICTOR. There's no such problem here.

SOLOMON. Unless we're gonna talk about a few pieces, then it wouldn't bother me, but to take the whole load without a paper is a...

VICTOR. All right, I'll get you some kind of statement from him; don't worry about it.

SOLOMON. That's definite; because even from high-class people you wouldn't believe the shenanigans—lawyers, college professors, television personalities—five hundred dollars they'll pay a lawyer to fight over a bookcase it's worth fifty cents—because you see, every-body wants to be number one, so...

VICTOR. I said I'd get you a statement. *(Indicates the room.)* Now what's the story?

SOLOMON. All right, so I'll tell you the story.

> *He looks to the dining room table, and points to it.*

For instance, you mention the dining room table. That's what they call Spanish Jacobean. Cost maybe twelve, thirteen hundred dollars.

I would say—1921, 22. I'm right?

VICTOR. Probably, ya.

SOLOMON. I see you're an intelligent man, so before I'll say another word, I ask you to remember—with used furniture you cannot be emotional.

VICTOR. *(Laughs.)* I haven't opened my mouth!

SOLOMON. I mean you're a policeman, I'm a furniture dealer, we both know this world—anything Spanish Jacobean you'll sell quicker a case of tuberculosis.

VICTOR. Why? That table's in beautiful condition.

SOLOMON. Officer, you're talking reality; you cannot talk reality with used furniture. They don't like that style, not only they don't like it, they hate, it. The same thing with that buffet there and that…

> *He starts to point elsewhere.*

VICTOR. You only want to take a few pieces, is that the ticket?

SOLOMON. *(Rising.)* Please, Officer, we're already talking too fast.

VICTOR. No-no, you're not going to walk off with the gravy and leave me with the bones. All or nothing or let's forget it. I told you on the phone it was a whole houseful.

SOLOMON. What're you in such a hurry? Talk a little bit, we'll see what happens. In a day they didn't build Rome.

> *He calculates worriedly for a moment, glancing again at the pieces he wants as he crosses R. a few steps.*

You see, what I had in mind—I would give you such a knockout price for these few pieces, that you…

VICTOR. That's *out.*

SOLOMON. Out!

VICTOR. I'm not running a department store. They're tearing the building down.

SOLOMON. Couldn't be better! We understand each other so… *(With his charm.)* —so there's no reason to be emotional.

> *Victor crosses L., sits against table. Pressed, nervous—Solomon crosses to records.*

These records go?

> *Picks up one.*

VICTOR. I might keep three or four.

SOLOMON. *(Reading a label.)* Look at that!—Gallagher and Shean!

VICTOR. *(With only half a laugh.)* You're not going to start playing them now!

SOLOMON. Who needs to play? I was on the same bill with Gallagher and Sheean maybe fifty theaters.

VICTOR. *(Surprised.)* You were an actor?

SOLOMON. An actor!—an acrobat; my whole family was acrobats.

> *Expanding with this first opening.*

You never heard "The Five Solomons"—may they rest in peace?

> *Points down toward edge of stage.*

I was the one on the bottom.

VICTOR. Funny—I never heard of a Jewish acrobat.

SOLOMON. What's the matter with Jacob, he wasn't a wrestler?—wrestled with the Angel?

> *Victor laughs.*

Jews been acrobats since the beginning of the world. I was a horse them days; drink, women, anything—on-the-go, on-the-go, nothing ever stopped me. Only life. Yes, my boy. *(Almost lovingly putting down the record.)* What do you know, Gallagher and Shean.

VICTOR. *(Rising. More intimately now, despite himself, but with no less persistence in keeping to the business.)* So where are we?

> *Solomon crosses R. few steps, then turns to him.*

SOLOMON. Tell me. What's with crime now? It's up, eh?

VICTOR. *(Crossing R. to U. L. of hassock.)* Yeah, it's up. It's up. Look, Mr. Solomon, let me make one thing clear, heh?—I'm not sociable.

SOLOMON. You're not.

VICTOR. No, I'm not; I'm not a businessman, I'm not good at conversations. So let's get to a price, and finish. Okay?

SOLOMON. *(At L. of Victor.)* You don't want we should be buddies.

VICTOR. That's exactly it.

SOLOMON. So we wouldn't be buddies!

Sighs.

But just so you'll know me a little better—I'm going to show you something.

> *Takes out a leather folder which he flips open and hands to Victor.*

There's my Discharge from the British Navy.

VICTOR. *(Looking at document.)* Huh!—what were you doing in the British Navy?

SOLOMON. Forget the British Navy. What does it say the date of birth?

VICTOR. "18"...?

> *Amazed, looks up at Solomon.*

You're almost ninety?

SOLOMON. Yes, my boy. I left Russia sixty-five years ago, I was twenty-four years old. And I smoked all my life. I drinked, and I loved every woman who would let me. So what do I need to steal from you?

VICTOR. Since when do people need a reason to steal?

SOLOMON. I never saw such a man in my life!

VICTOR. Oh, yes, you did. Now you going to give me a figure or...?

> *Solomon is actually frightened because he can't get a hook into Victor and fears losing the good pieces.*

SOLOMON. How can I give you a figure?—you don't trust one word I say!

VICTOR. *(With a strained laugh.)* I never saw you before, what're you asking me to trust you?!

SOLOMON. *(With a gesture of disgust.)* But how am I going to start to talk to you? I'm sorry; here you can't be a policeman—if you want to do business a little bit you gotta believe or you can't do it. I'm...I'm...look, forget it.

> *He goes L. toward his briefcase.*

VICTOR. *(Astonished.)* What are you doing?

SOLOMON. *(Turns R. of D. chair.)* I can't work this way. I'm too old every time I open my mouth you should practically call me a thief.

31

VICTOR. Who called you a thief?

SOLOMON. No—I don't need it. I don't want it in my shop. *(Wagging a finger into Victor's face.)* And don't forget it—I never gave you a price, and look what you did to me. You see?—I never gave you a price!

> *Crosses L.*

VICTOR. *(Angering. Crossing L. to R. of piano bench.)* Well, what did you come here for—to do me a favor? What are you talking about?

> *Solomon turns D. of table.*

SOLOMON. Mister, I pity you! What is the matter with you people! You're worse than my daughter!—Nothing in the world you believe, nothing you respect—how can you live? You think that's such a smart thing? That's so hard, what you're doing? Let me give you a piece advice—it's not that you can't believe nothing, that's not so hard—it's that you still got to believe it. That's hard. And if you can't do that, my friend—you're a dead man!

> *Picks up hat from table, puts it on.*

VICTOR. *(Crossing L. to R. of D. chair. Chastened despite himself.)* Oh, Solomon, come on, will you?

SOLOMON. *(Picking up brief case, crossing toward door.)* No-no… you got a certain problem with this furniture but you don't want to listen so how can I talk?

VICTOR. I'm listening!—For Christ's sake, what do you want me to do, get down on my knees?

> *Solomon turns at door.*

I'm listening.

> *Solomon puts down his briefcase, hat, cane and cigar on table, takes out a wrinkled tape measure from his jacket pocket.*

SOLOMON. Okay, come here. I realize you are a factual person, but some facts are funny.

> *He stretches the tape measure across the depth of a buffet against L. wall.*

What does that read?

> *Crosses to Victor, showing him at D. of table. Victor comes to him.*

VICTOR. *(Reads.)* Forty inches. So?

SOLOMON. My boy, the bedroom doors in a modern apartment house are thirty, thirty-two inches maximum. So you can't get this in—

> *Puts tape back in overcoat pocket.*

VICTOR. What about the old houses?

SOLOMON. *(With a desperation growing.)* All I'm trying to tell you is that my possibilities are smaller!

VICTOR. Well, can't I ask a question?

SOLOMON. I'm giving you architectural facts! Listen...

> *Wiping his face, he seizes on the library table, going to c.*

You got there, for instance, a library table. That's a solid beauty. But go find me a modern apartment with a library. If they would build old hotels, I could sell this but they only build new hotels. People don't live like this no more. This stuff is from another world. So I'm trying to give you a modern viewpoint. Because the price of used furniture is nothing but a viewpoint, and if you wouldn't understand the viewpoint is impossible to understand the price.

VICTOR. *(Crossing r. to him.)* So what's the viewpoint—that it's all worth nothing?

SOLOMON. That's what you said, I didn't say that. The chairs is worth something, the chiffoniers, the bed, the harp...

VICTOR. Okay, let's forget it, you're not going to leave me with...

SOLOMON. What're you jumping?

VICTOR. Good God, are you going to make me an offer or not!

SOLOMON. *(Walking away with a hand at his temple.)* Boy, oh boy, oh boy—you must've arrested a million people by now.

> *Turns back to him.*

VICTOR. Nineteen in twenty-eight years.

SOLOMON. So what are you so hard on me?

VICTOR. Because you talk about everything but money and I don't know what the hell you're up to.

SOLOMON. *(Raising a finger.)* We will now talk money.

VICTOR. Great. I mean you can't blame me—every time you open your mouth the price seems to go down.

SOLOMON. My boy, the price didn't change since I walked in.

VICTOR. That's even better! So what's the price?

> *Solomon glances about, his wit failed, a sunk look coming over his face as he sits in armchair.*

What's going on? ...What's bothering you?

SOLOMON. I'm sorry, I shouldn't have come. I thought it would be a few pieces but...

> *Sunk, he presses his fingers into his eyes.*

It's too much for me.

VICTOR. Well, what'd you come for? I told you it was the whole house.

SOLOMON. *(Protesting.)* You called me so I came! What should I do, lay down and die?

> *Striving again to save it.*

—Look, I want very much to make you an offer, the only question is...

> *He breaks off as though fearful of saying something.*

VICTOR. *(Crossing L. to table.)* This is a hell of a note...

SOLOMON. Listen, it's a terrible temptation to me! But... *(As though throwing himself on Victor's understanding.)* ...you see, I'll tell you the truth; you must have looked in a very old phone book;

> *Victor crosses U. to L. of phonograph, puts chin in hand.*

A couple of years ago already I cleaned out my store. Except a few English andirons I got left, I sell when I need a few dollars. I figure, I was eighty, eighty-five, it was time already. But I waited—and nothing happened—I even moved out of my apartment. I'm living in the back of the store with a hot-plate. But nothing happened. I'm still practically a hundred percent—not a hundred but I feel very well. And I figured maybe you got a couple nice pieces—not that the rest can't be sold but it could take a year, year and half. For me that's a big bet.

> *In conflict, he looks around.*

34

The trouble is I love to work; I love it, but— *(Giving up.)* I don't know what to tell you.

VICTOR. *(Crossing R.)* Well, all right, let's forget it then.

SOLOMON. What're you jumping?

VICTOR. *(At D. R. of hassock.)* Well, are you in or out?

SOLOMON. *(Rising.)* How do I know where I am? You see, it's also this particular furniture—the average person he'll take one look, it'll make him very nervous.

VICTOR. Solomon, you're starting again.

SOLOMON. I'm not bargaining with you!

VICTOR. Why'll it make him nervous?

SOLOMON. Because he knows it's never gonna break.

VICTOR. *(Not in bad humor, but clinging to his senses; sitting on hassock.)* Oh, come on, will you?—have a little mercy.

SOLOMON. My boy, you don't know the psychology!—If it wouldn't break there is no more possibilities. For instance, you take—

Crosses L. to table.

—this table...Listen!

He bangs the table.

You can't move it. A man sits down to such a table he knows not only he's married, he's got to stay married—there is no more possibilities.

Victor laughs. Solomon crosses R. to L. of Victor.

You're laughing, I'm telling you the factual situation. What is the key word today?—Disposable. The more you can throw it away the more it's beautiful. The car, the furniture, the wife, the children—everything has to be disposable. Because you see the main thing today is—shopping. Years ago a person, he was unhappy, didn't know what to do with himself—he go to church, start a revolution—*something*. Today you're unhappy? Can't figure it out?—what is the salvation?—go shopping.

VICTOR. *(Laughing.)* You're terrific, I have to give you credit.

SOLOMON. I'm telling you the truth!—If they would close the stores for six months in this country there would be from coast to coast a regular massacre. With this kind of furniture the shopping is over, it's finished, there's no more possibilities, you *got* it, you see? So you got a problem here.

VICTOR. *(Laughing.)* Solomon, you are one of the greatest.

SOLOMON. *(Smiling.)* What, the greatest?

VICTOR. I used to sell encyclopedias, door-to-door, and you know what that is…

SOLOMON. *(Happily fascinated.)* You don't say! You sold…?

VICTOR. Oh yeah; I was top man in the southern part of West-chester County, but you make me look like a…

SOLOMON. So why did you give it up?

VICTOR. *(With the amused smile.)* I couldn't stand the bullshit.

> *Solomon backs away a step.*

I'm not criticizing you, I admire it. I'm serious. Sometimes I wish I was that way myself. But I'm way ahead of you, it's not going to work.

SOLOMON. *(Offended.)* What "work"? I don't know how much time I got. What is so terrible if I say that? The trouble is, you're such a young fella you don't understand these things…

VICTOR. I understand very well, I know what you're up against— I'm not so young.

SOLOMON. *(Scoffing.)* What are you, forty? Forty-five?

VICTOR. I'm going to be fifty.

SOLOMON. *(Crossing D. to piano bench.)* Fifty! You're a baby boy!

VICTOR. Some baby.

SOLOMON. *(Sitting bench.)* My God, if I was fifty…! I got married I was seventy-five.

VICTOR. Go on.

SOLOMON. What are you talking?—She's still living by Eighth Avenue over there. See, that's why I like to stay liquid, because if she'll get her hands on this I don't want it… Birds she loves. She's living there with maybe a hundred birds. She gives you a plate of soup it's got feathers—I didn't work all my life for them birds.

VICTOR. I appreciate your problems, Mr. Solomon, but I don't have to pay for them;

Stands.

I've got no more time.

SOLOMON. *(Rising, holding up a restraining hand—desperately.)* I'm going to buy it!

> *He has shocked himself, and glances around at the towering masses of furniture.*

I mean I'll…I'll have to live, that's all, I'll make up my mind! I'll buy it.

Victor is affected as Solomon's fear comes through to him.

VICTOR. We're talking about everything now. *(?)*

SOLOMON. *(Angrily.)* Everything, everything! *(Going to his portfolio on the dining room table.)* I'll figure it up, I'll give you a very nice price, and you'll be a happy man.

VICTOR. That I doubt.

> *Solomon takes a hard-boiled egg out of the portfolio and cracks it on his knuckles.*

What's this now, lunch?

SOLOMON. *(Peeling shell off of egg.)* You give me such an argument I'm hungry! I'm not supposed to get too hungry.

VICTOR. *(Crossing R., sits on sofa.)* Brother.

SOLOMON. You want me to starve to death? I'm going to be very quick here.

VICTOR. Boy—I picked a number!

> *Solomon throws shells into briefcase.*

SOLOMON. There wouldn't be a little salt, I suppose.

VICTOR. I'm not going running for salt now.

SOLOMON. Please, don't be blue. I'm going to knock you off your feet with the price, you'll see.

> *He eats the egg. He now faces the furniture, and half to himself—the pad and pencil poised.*

I'm going to go here like an IBM.

> *He goes quickly to start estimating to his pad.*

VICTOR. That's all right, take it easy. As long as you're serious.

SOLOMON. *(Crossing U.)* Thank you.

He jots down a figure. He goes to the next piece, jots down another figure.

VICTOR. *(After a moment.)* You really got married at seventy-five?

SOLOMON. *(At U. L. of phonograph.)* What's so terrible?

VICTOR. No, I think it's terrific. But what was the point?

SOLOMON. What's the point at twenty-five? You can't die twenty-six?

VICTOR. *(Laughs softly.)* I guess so, ya.

SOLOMON. *(Crossing R. above bedstead to bedroom.)* It's the same like second-hand furniture, you see; the whole thing is a viewpoint. It's a mental world.

> *Opens door.*

Seventy-five I got married, fifty-one, and twenty-two.

> *Closes door.*

VICTOR. You're kidding.

SOLOMON. *(As he works, writing on the pad.)* I wish!

> *He works, jotting his estimate of each piece on the pad, opening drawers, touching everything.*

VICTOR. You're a hell of a guy.

> *Smiling with the encouragement, Solomon turns to Victor, crosses to U. L. of sofa.*

SOLOMON. You know it's a funny thing. It's so long since I took on such a load like this—you forget what kind of life it puts into you. To take out a pencil again…it's a regular injection. Because I'll tell you the truth, my telephone you could use for a ladle, it wouldn't interfere with nothing. But when you called me, well, I don't want to take up your time. But—I want to thank you; very much.

> *Points to Victor.*

I'm going to take good care of you, I mean it. I can open that?

VICTOR. Sure, anything.

SOLOMON. *(Goes to the armoire.)* Some of them had a mirror…

> *He opens the D. door of armoire and a rolled-up fur rug falls out. It is about three by five.*

What's this?

VICTOR. God knows. I guess it's a rug.

SOLOMON. *(Throwing it across back of sofa.)* No-no—that's a lap robe. Like for a car.

VICTOR. Say that's right, ya. When they went driving. God, I haven't seen that in…

SOLOMON. You had a chauffeur?

VICTOR. Ya, we had a chauffeur.

> *Their eyes meet. Solomon looks at him as though Victor were coming into focus. Now Solomon turns back to the armoire, opens U. door.*

SOLOMON. Look a that!

> *Takes down an opera hat from the shelf within.*

My God!

> *He puts it on, looks into the interior mirror that is on the inside of D. door.*

What a world!

> *Turns to Victor.*

He must've been some sporty guy!

VICTOR. *(Smiling.)* You look pretty good!

SOLOMON. *(Behind sofa.)* And from all this he could go so broke?

VICTOR. Why not? Sure. Took five weeks. Less.

SOLOMON. You don't say. And he couldn't make a comeback. *(?)*

VICTOR. Well, some men don't bounce, you know.

SOLOMON. *(A grunt.)* Hmm! So what did he do?

VICTOR. Nothing. Just sat here. Listened to the radio.

SOLOMON. But what did he do? What…?

VICTOR. Well, now and then he was making change at the Automat. Toward the end he was delivering telegrams.

SOLOMON. *(With grief and wonder.)* You don't say. And how much he had?

VICTOR. Oh…couple of million, I guess.

SOLOMON. My God. What was the matter with him?

VICTOR. *(Rising, crossing L., turns at D. L. of phonograph.)* —Well, my mother died around the same time—I guess that didn't help. Some men just don't bounce, that's all.

SOLOMON. Listen, I can tell you bounces—I went busted 1932; then 1923 they also knocked me out; the Panic of 1904, 1898... But to lay down like *that*...

VICTOR. Well, you're different. He believed in it.

SOLOMON. What he believed?

VICTOR. The system, the whole thing.—He thought it was his fault, I guess. You—you come in with your song and dance, it's all a gag—you're a hundred and fifty years old, you tell your jokes, people fall in love with you and you walk away with their furniture.

SOLOMON. That's not nice.

> *Crosses R. to armoire, puts hat back, closes doors.*

VICTOR. Don't shame me, will ya?—What do you say? You don't need to look anymore, you know what I've got here.

> *Solomon is clearly at the end of his delaying resources, he looks about slowly; as he crosses up to U. of sofa the furniture seems to loom over him like a threat or a promise. His eyes climb up to the edges of the ceiling, his hands grasping one another.*

What are you afraid of?—It'll keep you busy.

> *Solomon looks at him, wanting even more reassurance.*

SOLOMON. You don't think it's foolish. *(?)*

VICTOR. Who knows what's foolish? You enjoy it...

SOLOMON. Listen, I love it...

VICTOR. ...So take it. You plan too much, you end up with nothing.

SOLOMON. *(Intimately. Crossing L. to armchair.)* I would like to tell you something. The last few months, I don't know what it is— she comes to me. You see, I had a daughter, she should rest in peace, she took her own life, a suicide...

VICTOR. When was this?

> *Solomon sits armchair. Victor crosses, sits chair R. of middle of table.*

40

SOLOMON. It was...1915—the latter part. But very beautiful, a lovely face, with large eyes—she was pure like the morning. And lately, I don't know what it is—I see her clear like I see you. And every night practically, I lay down to go to sleep, so she sits there. And you can't help it, you ask yourself—what happened? What happened? Maybe I could have said something to her...maybe I did say something...it's all... It's not that I'll die, you can't be afraid of that. But...I'll tell you the truth—a minute ago I mentioned I had three wives...

Slight pause. His fear rises.

Just this minute I realize I had four. Isn't that terrible? See, that's what I mean—it's impossible to know what is important. Here I'm sitting with you...and...and... What for? Not that I don't want it, I want it, but... You see, all my life I was a terrible fighter—you could never take nothing from me; I pushed, I pulled, I struggled in six different countries, I nearly got killed a couple times, and it's... It's like now I'm sitting here talking to you and I tell you it's a dream, it's a dream! You see, you can't imagine it because...

VICTOR. I understand it very well.

SOLOMON. What do you understand?

VICTOR. I think it's what you just said—it's impossible to know what's important. The big decision is always the one you don't realize you're making—till the results start coming in. And then you're stuck with it.

SOLOMON. Why?—you're healthy, you got such a nice... *(Realizing.)* Your wife is all right?

VICTOR. Oh ya, she's a terrific woman—best piece of luck I ever had. But like—when we started out, the one important thing was to live the life we wanted, not the rat race. But I don't think there is anything else. Unless you've got some kind of talent—but otherwise it's three feeds a day, and you make a kid for the Army, and then you lose your hair, and pack it in.

Rising, crossing R. above phonograph to U. of sofa.

Not that I'm complaining, but finally there's just no respect for anything but money. You try to stay above it; but you shovel it out the window and it creeps in under the door. It all ends up—she wants.

She wants. And I can't blame her for it. Like we've got people in our apartment house, ignorant knuckleheads, they can hardly write their names; but last month a couple knocks on the door to offer us their old refrigerator, buy a new one every couple of years. They know what I make, y'see? and it's that friendly viciousness, just to show who's on top. And things like that are eating her out...

SOLOMON. What does she want, a police commissioner? An honest cop is a...is a... *(Struggles for the complimentary term.)*

VICTOR. He's a jerk. Took me fourteen years to get the goddamn stripes because I wouldn't kiss ass.—Which we were always in perfect agreement about, but you end up... Like I'm supposed to retire now...

SOLOMON. What're you going to do?

VICTOR. That's not really the problem—I'll do something. *(Crossing to R. of sofa.)* It's that it's hard to find the point in it anymore—the whole thing. For years I thought it would mean some kind of freedom. Study science again; something interesting. But that'll take three, four years in school, and she's not in the mood for sacrifice anymore, and I'm not sure I am either.

> *Crosses to D. of sofa.*

So what's left?—Go sell something, shoot the bull one way or another—which is just what I was trying to avoid. There are days when I can't even remember what I was trying to do. Except, there was an idea we had, that...

SOLOMON. No, you see—you make one mistake. A man can think whatever he want to think, but he should never...

VICTOR. *(Crossing up to R. of hassock.)* ...Forget about the money.

SOLOMON. What've you got against money?

VICTOR. Nothing, I'm all for it—I just didn't want to lay down my life for it, that's all. *(Sitting on sofa.)* But you lay it down another way...and you're a damn fool in the bargain. I guess it's the old story—you can do anything, just make sure you win.—Like my brother; years ago, I was living here with the old man, and he used to contribute five dollars a month. A month, and a successful doctor. I had to drop out of school to keep the guy from starving to death. Point I'm making, though, is that the few times he'd come

42

around, the expression on the old man's face—you'd think God walked in. The respect, you know what I mean? And why not? Why not?

SOLOMON. Well sure, he had the power.

VICTOR. Now you said it—if you got that you got it all—you're even lovable! *(Rising to U. of hassock.)* Well, what do you say? Give me the price.

SOLOMON. *(Rising. Slight pause.)* I will give you eleven hundred dollars.

> *Slight pause.*

VICTOR. For everything?

SOLOMON. *(In a breathless way.)* Everything.

> *Slight pause. Victor looks around at the stuff.*

I want it so I'm giving you a good price. Believe me, you will never do better. I want it; I made up my mind.

> *Victor continues staring at the stuff. Solomon takes out a common envelope and removes a wad of bills.*

Here…I'll pay you now.

> *He readies a bill to start counting it out.*

VICTOR. It's that I have to split it, see…

SOLOMON. All right…so I'll make out a receipt for you and I'll put down six hundred dollars.

> *Starts L. toward briefcase.*

VICTOR. No-no…

SOLOMON. *(Turns back.)* Why not? He took from you so take from him. If you want, I'll put down four hundred.

VICTOR. No, I don't want to do that.

> *Slight pause.*

—I'll call you tomorrow.

SOLOMON. *(Smiles.)* All right; with God's help if I'm there tomorrow I'll answer the phone. If I wouldn't be…

> *Slight pause.*

Then I wouldn't be.

VICTOR. *(Annoyed, but wanting to believe.)* Don't start that again, will you?

SOLOMON. *(Crossing back to Victor.)* Look, you convinced me, so I want it—so what should I do?

VICTOR. *I* convinced *you.*

SOLOMON. *(Very distressed.)* Absolutely you convinced me. You saw it—the minute I looked at it I was going to walk out!

VICTOR. *(Cutting him off, angered at his own indecision.)* Ah, the hell with it.

> *Holds out his hand.*

Give it to me.

SOLOMON. *(Wanting Victor's good will.)* Please, don't be blue.

VICTOR. Oh, it all stinks. *(Jabbing forth his hand.)* Come on.

SOLOMON. *(With a bill raised over Victor's hand—protesting.)* What stinks? You should be happy—now you can buy her a nice coat, take her to Florida, maybe…

VICTOR. *(Nodding ironically.)* Right, right!—we'll all be happy now. Give it to me.

> *Solomon shakes his head and counts bills into his hand, Victor turns his head and looks at the piled walls of furniture.*

SOLOMON. There's one hundred; two hundred; three hundred; four hundred… Take my advice, buy her a nice fur coat your troubles'll be over…

VICTOR. I know all about it. Come on.

SOLOMON. So you got there four, so I'm giving you…five, six, seven… I mean it's already in the Bible, the rat race. The minute she laid her hand on the apple, that's it.

VICTOR. I never read the Bible. Come on.

SOLOMON. If you'll read it you'll see—there's always a rat race, you can't stay out of it. So you got there seven, so now I'm giving you…

> *A man enters, crosses to D. of dining room table. In his mid-fifties, well-barbered, hatless, in a camel's-hair coat, very healthy complexion. A look of sharp intelligence on his face. Victor, seeing past Solomon, starts slightly with shock, with-*

drawing his hand from the next bill which Solomon is about to lay in it. He is suddenly flushed, his voice oddly high and boyish.

VICTOR. Walter!

Walter comes to Victor with extended hand, and with a reserve of warmth, but a stiff smile

WALTER. How are you, kid?

Solomon has moved to L. of Walter. Victor shifts the money to his left as he shakes.

VICTOR. God, I never expected you.

WALTER. *(Of the money—half-humorously.)* Sorry I'm late. What are you doing?

VICTOR. *(Fighting a treason to himself, thus taking on a strained humorous air.)* I…I just sold it.

WALTER. Good! How much?

VICTOR. *(As though absolutely certain now he has been had.)* Ah…eleven hundred.

WALTER. *(In a dead voice shorn of comment.)* Oh. Well, good.

He turns rather deliberately—but not overly so—to Solomon.

For everything?

SOLOMON. *(With an energized voice that braves everything, he comes to Walter, his hand extended.)* I'm very happy to meet you, Doctor! My name is Gregory Solomon.

The look on Walter's face is rather amused, but his reserve has possibilities of accusation.

WALTER. How do you do?

He shakes Solomon's hand.

CURTAIN ACT I

ACT II

The action is continuous and it is preferable to play without an intermission. However, if one is required, the curtain rises on Walter just releasing Solomon's hand and turning about to face Victor. His posture is reserved, stiffened by traditional control over a nearly fierce curiosity. His grin is disciplined and rather hard, but the eyes are warm and combative.

WALTER. How's Esther?

VICTOR. Fine. Should be here any minute.

WALTER. Here?—Good! And what's Richard doing?

Solomon crosses, sits D. chair which is R. of table.

VICTOR. He's at M.I.T.

WALTER. No kidding!—M.I.T.!

Victor nods.

VICTOR. Ya. They gave him a full scholarship.

WALTER. *(Dispelling his surprise.)* What do you know! *(With a wider smile, and embarrassed warmth.)* You're proud.

VICTOR. I guess so. They put him in the Honors Program.

WALTER. Really. That's wonderful.—You don't mind my coming, do you?

VICTOR. No! I called you a couple of times.

WALTER. Yes, my nurse told me. What's Richard interested in?

VICTOR. Science. So far, anyway. *(With security.)* How are yours?

Moving below Victor to sofa, Walter breaks the confrontation.

WALTER. I suppose Jean turned out best—but I don't think you ever saw her.

VICTOR. I never did, no.

WALTER. The *Times* gave her quite a spread last fall. She's a pretty fair designer.

46

Crosses u. to standing lamp.

VICTOR. *(At D. of armchair.)* Oh?—That's great. And the boys? They in school?

WALTER. They often are—I hardly see them, Vic.

Abruptly laughs, refusing his own embarrassment.

With all the unsolved mysteries in the world they're investigating the guitar. But what the hell...I've given up worrying about them. *(Glancing at the furniture.)* I'd forgotten how much he had up here. *(Crossing to u. R. of sofa.)* —There's your radio!

VICTOR. *(Smiling with him.)* I know, I saw it.

Walter looks up at the ceiling where Victor pointed earlier. Both laugh as Victor crosses to u. of sofa. Then he glances with open feeling at Victor.

WALTER. Long time.

VICTOR. Ya.

Walks away L. a few steps.

How's Dorothy?

WALTER. *(Cryptically.)* She's all right, I guess.

He moves u., then crosses L., glancing at the things.

Looking forward to seeing Esther again; she still writing poetry?

VICTOR. No, not for years now.

SOLOMON. He's got a very nice wife. We met.

WALTER. *(At L. of phonograph; surprised, as though at something intrusive.)* Oh?

He turns back to the furniture. With affection...

Well. Same old junk, isn't it?

VICTOR. *(Downing a greater protest.)* I wouldn't say that. Some of it isn't bad.

SOLOMON. One or two very nice things, Doctor. We came to a very nice agreement.

VICTOR. *(With an implied rebuke. Crossing L. to c.)* I never thought you'd show up; I guess we'd better start all over again...

WALTER. *(Crossing D. to L. of Victor.)* Oh, no-no, I don't want to foul up your deal.

SOLOMON. *(Rising.)* Excuse me, Doctor—better you should take what you want now than we'll argue later. What did you want?

WALTER. *(Surprised, turns to Victor.)* Oh, I didn't want anything. I came by to say hello, that's all.

VICTOR. I see.

> *Fending off Walter's apparent gesture, with an over-quick movement toward the oar which is u. l.*

I found your oar, if you want it.

WALTER. Oar?

> *As Victor draws it out from behind furniture and brings it to him.*

Hah!

> *He receives the oar, looks up its great length and laughs, hefting it.*

I must have been out of my mind!

SOLOMON. Excuse me, Doctor; if you want the oar...

WALTER. *(Standing the oar on end before Solomon, who grasps it in surprise.)* Don't get excited, I don't want it.

SOLOMON. No. I was going to say—a personal thing like that I have no objection.

> *Victor returns oar to u. l.*

WALTER. *(Annoyed, despite himself—he half-laughs.)* That's very generous of you.

VICTOR. *(Apologizing for Solomon.)* I threw in everything—I never thought you'd get here.

WALTER. *(With a strained over-agreeableness, looking around. Crossing r. to sofa.)* Sure, that's all right. What are you taking?

VICTOR. *(At l. of phonograph.)* Nothing, really. Esther might want a lamp or something like that.

SOLOMON. He's not interested, you see; he's a modern person, what are you going to do?

WALTER. You're not taking the harp?

VICTOR. *(With a certain guilt.)* Well, nobody plays… You take it, if you like…

SOLOMON. You'll excuse me, Doctor—the harp, please, that's another story…

WALTER. *(Laughs—archly amused and put-out.)* You don't mind if I make a suggestion, do you?

SOLOMON. Doctor please, don't be offended, I only…

WALTER. *(With a steady, iron smile.)* Why don't you just relax? We're only talking. We haven't seen each other in a long time.

SOLOMON. Couldn't be better; I'm very sorry.

> *Walter crosses to harp. Solomon crosses R. to C.*

VICTOR. We wouldn't have room for it anyway.

WALTER. *(Touching the harp.)* Kind of a pity—this was Grandpa's wedding present, you know.

VICTOR. *(Looking with surprise at the harp.)* Say—that's right!

WALTER. *(To Solomon.)* What are you giving him for this?

SOLOMON. I didn't itemize—one price for everything. Maybe three hundred dollars.—That sounding board is cracked, you know.

VICTOR. *(To Walter.)* You want it?

SOLOMON. *(Crossing R. to Victor.)* Please, Victor, I hope you're not going to take that away from me. *(To Walter as he crosses to D. L. of sofa.)* Look, Doctor, I'm not trying to fool you—the harp is the heart and soul of the deal. I realize it belonged to your mother, but…but like I tried to tell *(To Victor.)* you before… *(To Walter.)* with used furniture you cannot be emotional.

WALTER. *(Looks at harp. To Victor, crossing up to U. of sofa.)* I guess it doesn't matter… Actually, I was wondering if he kept any of Mother's evening gowns. Did he?

VICTOR. I haven't really gone through it all…

SOLOMON. *(Raising a finger, eagerly.)* Wait, wait, I think I can help you.

> *He goes to an armoire he had earlier looked into, and opens it.*

WALTER. She had some spectacular…

SOLOMON. *(Drawing out a gown elaborately embroidered in gold.)* Is this what you mean?

WALTER. *(Crossing D. to behind sofa.)* Yes, that's the stuff! *(Taking a gown from Solomon.)* Isn't that beautiful!—Say, I think she wore this at my wedding!

> *Holds it up.*

Sure! You remember this?

VICTOR. *(Surprised at this emotion.)* What do you want with it?

WALTER. I thought Jeannie might make something new out of the material. I'd like her to wear something of Mother's.

VICTOR. *(A new, surprising idea.)* Oh! Fine, that's a nice idea.

SOLOMON. *(Laying a second gown on the couch.)* Take, take—they're beautiful.

> *Walter puts first dress on back of sofa, picks up dress Solomon has just put there.*

WALTER. *(Suddenly glancing about.)* …What happened to the piano?

VICTOR. Oh, we sold that while I was still in school. We lived on it for a long time.

WALTER. *(Very interestedly.)* I never knew that.

VICTOR. Sure. And the silver.

WALTER. Of course! Stupid of me not to remember that.

VICTOR. *(A slight rebuke.)* Why? Why should you?

WALTER. I suppose you know—you've gotten to look a great deal like Dad.

VICTOR. *I* do?

WALTER. It's very striking. And your voice is very much like his.

VICTOR. I know; it has that sound to me, sometimes. *(Indicating Solomon, crossing R. to D. R. of armchair.)* Maybe we'd better settle this now.

WALTER. Yes, go ahead!—

> *Walter walks U. few steps, looking at the furniture. Solomon indicates the money Victor holds.*

SOLOMON. Don't worry. We didn't waste a minute so, gentle-men...you got there seven...

WALTER. *(Oblivious of Solomon, unable to, so to speak, settle for the status quo.)* Wonderful to see you looking so well.

VICTOR. *(The new interruption seems odd—observing more than speaking.)* You do too, you look great.

WALTER. I ski a lot; and I ride nearly every morning... You know, I started to call you a dozen times this year... *(Breaks off—indicating Solomon.)* Finish up, I'll talk to you later.

SOLOMON. So now I'm going to give you...

    A bill is poised over Victor's hand.

VICTOR. That price all right with you?

WALTER. *(Crossing D. and below sofa to L. of it.)* Oh, I don't want to interfere—It's just that I dealt with these fellows when I split up Dorothy's and my stuff last year, and I found...

VICTOR. *(From an earlier impression.)* You're not divorced, are you?

WALTER. *(A nervous shot of laughter.)* Yes!

    Esther enters on his line; she is carrying a suit in a plastic
    wrapper.

ESTHER. *(At D. R. of dining room table. Off-guard, surprised.)* Walter! For heaven's sake!

WALTER. *(Crossing L. above bench. Eagerly coming to her, shaking her hand, his voice nervous, quiet.)* How are you, Esther!

ESTHER. *(Between her disapproval and fascinated surprise.)* What are you doing here?

WALTER. You've hardly changed!

ESTHER. *(With a charged laugh, conflicted with herself.)* Oh, go on now!

WALTER. *(To Victor.)* You son of a gun, she looks twenty-five!

VICTOR. *(Watching for Esther's reaction.)* I know!

ESTHER. *(Crossing R., puts suit on back of sofa. Flattered and of-fended too.)* Oh, stop it, Walter!

WALTER. But you do, honestly; you look marvelous.

SOLOMON. It's that suit, you see? What did I tell you, it's a very beautiful suit.

Solomon sits armchair. Victor laughs a little as she looks to Solomon, conflicted by his compliment.

ESTHER. *(With mock-affront—to Victor.)* What are you laughing at?—It is.

Esther sits sofa.

VICTOR. You looked so surprised, that's all…

ESTHER. *(Taking cigarette out of purse.)* Well, I'm not used to walking into all these compliments!

Walter crosses R. to her, lights her cigarette.

WALTER. *(Suddenly recalling—eagerly.)* Say…! I'm sorry I didn't know I'd be seeing you when I left the house this morning—I'd have brought you some lovely Indian bracelets. I got a whole boxful from Bombay.

Esther is still not focused on Walter, sizing him up.

ESTHER. How do you come to…?

Puts purse on sofa.

WALTER. I operated on this big textile guy and he keeps sending me things. He sent me this coat, in fact…

ESTHER. I was noticing it. That's gorgeous material.

WALTER. Isn't it? Two gallstones.

He laughs with a certain shy victory.

ESTHER. *(Her impression lingering for the instant.)* How's Dorothy?—Did I hear you saying you were…?

WALTER. *(Very seriously.)* We're divorced, ya. Last winter.

ESTHER. I'm sorry to hear that.

WALTER. It was coming a long time. We're both much better off— we're almost friendly now.

ESTHER. Oh, stop that, you dog.

WALTER. *(With naive excitement.)* It's true!

ESTHER. Look, I'm for the woman, so don't hand me that. *(To Victor—seeing the money in his hand.)* Have you settled everything?

VICTOR. Just about, I guess…

WALTER. I was just telling Victor— *(To Victor.)* when we broke up our home… *(Crossing up to D. R. of side table R. of armchair. To Solomon.)* You ever hear of Spitzer and Fox?

SOLOMON. Thirty years I know Spitzer and Fox. Bert Fox worked for me maybe ten, twelve years.

WALTER. They did my appraisal.

SOLOMON. They're good boys. Spitzer is not as good as Fox, but between the two you're in good hands.

WALTER. Yes. That's why I…

SOLOMON. Spitzer is vice president of the Appraisers' Association.

WALTER. I see. The point I'm making…

SOLOMON. I used to be president.

WALTER. Really.

SOLOMON. Oh yes. I made it all ethical.

WALTER. *(Trying to keep a straight face—and Victor as well.)* Did you.

> *Victor suddenly bursts out laughing, which sets off Walter and Esther, and a warmth springs up among them.*

SOLOMON. *(Smiling, but insistent.)* What's so funny? Listen, before me was a jungle—you wouldn't laugh so much.

> *Walter moves away U., impatient to get on with it.*

I put in all the rates, what we charge, you know—I made it a profession, like doctors, lawyers—used to be it was a regular snakepit. Today, you got nothing to worry—all the members are hundred percent ethical.

WALTER. *(Crossing D. to U. L. of sofa,)* Well, that was a good deed, Mister Solomon—but I think you can do a little better on this furniture.

ESTHER. *(To Victor, who has money in his hand.)* How much has he offered?

VICTOR. *(Embarrassed, but braving it quite well.)* …Eleven hundred.

ESTHER. *(Distressed, with a transcendent protest.)* Oh, I think that's… isn't that very low?

She looks to Walter's confirmation.

WALTER. *(Familiarly.)* Come on, Solomon—he's been risking his life for you every day; be generous…

SOLOMON. *(To Esther.)* That's a real brother! Wonderful; *(To Walter.)* but you can call anybody you like—Spitzer and Fox, Joe Brody, Paul Cavallo, Morris White—I know them all and I know what they'll tell you.

VICTOR. *(Striving to retain some assurance—to Esther.)* See, the point he was making about it…

SOLOMON. *(To Esther, raising his finger.)* Listen to him because he…

VICTOR. *(Crossing R. to D. of phono records. To Solomon.)* Hold it one second, will you? *(To Esther and Walter.)* Not that I'm saying it's true, but he claims a lot of it is too big to get into the new apartments.

ESTHER. *(Rising, crossing up to U. L. of sofa. Half-laughing.)* You believe that?!

WALTER. *(Crossing D., to R. of sofa.)* I don't know, Esther, Spitzer and Fox said the same thing.

ESTHER. Walter, the city is full of big, old apartments. *(!)*

SOLOMON. Darling, why don't you leave it to the boys?

ESTHER. *(Suppressing an outburst.)* I wish you wouldn't order me around, Mister Solomon! *(To Walter, protesting.)* Those two bureaus alone are worth a couple of hundred dollars!

WALTER. *(Delicately.)* Maybe I oughtn't interfere…

ESTHER. Why?! *(Of Solomon.)* Don't let him bulldoze you…

SOLOMON. My dear girl, you're talking without a basis…

ESTHER. *(Slashing.)* I don't like this kind of dealing, Mr. Solomon! I just don't like it!

> *Victor crosses L. to R. of dining room table. She is near tears. A pause. She turns hack to Walter, crossing D. few steps—L. of sofa.*

This money is very important to us, Walter.

WALTER. *(Crossing D., sitting D. arm of sofa. Chastised.)* Yes, I… I'm sorry, Esther.

He looks about.

Well…if it was mine…

ESTHER. Why? It's yours as much as Victor's.

WALTER. Oh, no, dear—I wouldn't take anything from this.

> *A pause.*

VICTOR. No, Walter, you get half.

WALTER. I wouldn't think of it, kid. I came by to say hello, that's all.

> *A pause. She is very moved.*

ESTHER. That's terrific, Walter. It's… Really, I…

VICTOR. Well, we'll talk about it.

WALTER. *(Rising, crossing L. to D. L. of hassock.)* No-no, Vic, you've earned it. It's yours.

VICTOR. *(Rejecting the implication.)* Why have I earned it? You take your share.

WALTER. Why don't we discuss it later? *(Crossing U. to Solomon.)* In my opinion…

SOLOMON. *(To Victor.)* So now you don't even have to split. *(To Victor and Walter.)* You're lucky they're tearing the building down—you got together, finally.

WALTER. *(At D. R. of side table. With delicacy, to Victor.)* …I would have said a minimum of three thousand dollars.

ESTHER. That's exactly what I had in mind! *(To Solomon.)* I was going to say thirty-five hundred dollars.

WALTER. In that neighborhood.

> *Silence. Solomon sits there holding back his comment, not looking at Victor, blinking with protest. Victor thinks for a moment, then turns to Solomon, and there is a wide discouragement in his voice.*

VICTOR. Well? What do you say?

SOLOMON. *(Spreading out his hands helplessly and outraged.)* What can I say? It's ridiculous. Why does he give you three thousand? What's the matter with five thousand, ten thousand?

WALTER. *(Crossing L. to Victor. Without criticism—to Victor.)* You should've gotten a couple of other estimates, you see, that's always the...

VICTOR. I've been calling you all week for just that reason, Walter, and you never came to the phone.

WALTER. *(Blushing.)* Why would that stop you from...?

VICTOR. I didn't think I had the right to do it alone—the nurse gave you my messages, didn't she?

WALTER. I've been terribly tied up—and I had no intention of taking anything for myself, so I assumed...

VICTOR. But how was I supposed to know that?

WALTER. *(With open self-reproach.)* Yes. Well, I...I beg your pardon.

    He decides to stop there.

SOLOMON. Excuse me, Doctor, but I can't understand you; first it's a lot of junk...

ESTHER. *(Crossing U. to D. R. of side table.)* Nobody called it a lot of junk!

SOLOMON. He called it a lot of junk, Esther, when he walked in here.

    Esther turns to Walter, puzzled and angry.

WALTER. *(Reacting to her look—to Solomon.)* Now just a minute...

SOLOMON. *(Rising with difficulty so Esther and Walter help him up.)* No, please, *(Indicating Victor.)* this is a factual man, so let's be factual.

ESTHER. Well, that's an awfully strange thing to say, Walter.

WALTER. I didn't mean it in that sense, Esther...

SOLOMON. Doctor, please—you said junk.

WALTER. *(Sharply—and there is an over-meaning of much greater anger in his tone.)* I didn't mean it in that sense, Mister Solomon! *(He controls himself—and half to Esther.)* When you've been brought up with things you tend to be sick of them... *(To Esther.)* That's all I meant.

SOLOMON. My dear man, if it was Louis Seize, Biedermeier, something like that, you wouldn't get sick.

WALTER. *(Pointing to a piece, and weakened by knowing he is exaggerating.)* Well, there happens to be a piece right over there in Biedermeier style!

SOLOMON. Biedermeier "style"! I got a hat it's in Borsalino style but it's not a Borsalino. *(To Victor.)* I mean he don't have to charge me to make an impression.

WALTER. Now what's that supposed to mean?

VICTOR. *(Crossing R. below hassock to sofa. With a refusal to dump Solomon.)* Well, what basis do you go on, Walter?

WALTER. *(Reddening but smiling.)* I don't know…it's a feeling, that's all.

ESTHER. *(There is ridicule.)* Well, on what basis do you take eleven hundred, dear?

VICTOR. *(Angered—and his manly leadership is suddenly in front.)* I simply felt it was probably more or less right!

ESTHER. *(Crossing L. to table, puts cigarette out in ashtray. As a refrain.)* Oh, God, here we go again. All right, throw it away…

SOLOMON. *(Indicating Victor.)* Please, Esther, he's not throwing nothing away—this man is no fool! *(To Walter as well.)* Excuse me, but this is not right to do to him!

WALTER. *(Bridling, but retaining his smile.)* Are you going to teach me what's right now?

> Walter crosses U., looking around at furniture. Esther crosses D., sits chair D. R. of table.

ESTHER. *(To Victor, expanding Walter's protest.)* Really!—I mean.

> Victor crosses up to S. R. of Solomon. Obeying Esther's protest for want of a certainty of his own, he touches Solomon's shoulder.

VICTOR. Mister Solomon…why don't you sit down in the bedroom for a few minutes and let us talk?

SOLOMON. Certainly, whatever you say. Only please, you made a very nice deal, you got no right to be ashamed… *(To Esther.)* Excuse me, I don't want to be personal.

ESTHER. *(Laughs angrily.)* He's fantastic!

VICTOR. *(Trying to get him going again.)* Why'n't you go inside?

57

SOLOMON. I'm going; I only want you to understand, Victor, that if it was a different kind of man *(Turning to Esther.)* I would say to you that he's got the money in his hand, so the deal is concluded.

WALTER. *(Crossing D. to L. of Solomon.)* He can't conclude any deal without me, Solomon; I'm half owner here.

SOLOMON. *(To Victor.)* You see?! What did I ask you the first thing I walked in here?—"Who is the owner?"

WALTER. Why do you confuse everything? I'm not making any claim, I merely...

SOLOMON. Then how do you come to interfere? He's got the money; I know the law!

WALTER. *(Angering with frustration.)* Now you stop being foolish! Just stop it! I've got the best lawyers in New York, so go inside and sit down.

VICTOR. Take it easy, Walter, come on, cut it out.

ESTHER. *(Striving to keep a light, amused tone.)* Why? He's perfectly right.

VICTOR. *(With a hard glance at her, moving toward bedroom with Solomon.)* Here, you better hold on to this money.

SOLOMON. No, that's yours; you hold...

> He sways. Esther rises, crosses to U. of piano bench. Victor grasps his R. arm. Walter crosses to Solomon's left and they help him to sit on the hassock.

WALTER. You all right?

SOLOMON. *(Dizzy, he grasps his head.)* Yes, yes, I'm...

WALTER. Let me look at you.

> He takes Solomon's left wrist, looking into his face. Solomon shifts money from his left hand to his right.

SOLOMON. I'm only a little tired, I didn't take my nap today.

WALTER. Come in here, lie down for a moment.

> He starts to help up Solomon.

SOLOMON. Don't worry about me, I'm... *(Pointing across at his portfolio.)* Please, Doctor, if you wouldn't mind—I got a Hershey's in there,

Walter hesitates to do his errand.

Helps me. In the portfolio.

> *Walter unwillingly goes L. to his portfolio which is on table and reaches into it.*

I'm a very healthy person, but a nap, you see, I have to have a…

> *Walter returns with the portfolio, taking out an orange.*

Not the orange—on the bottom is a Hershey's.

> *Walter puts orange back, takes out a Hershey bar.*

That's a boy.

> *Walter puts portfolio on side table R. of armchair.*

WALTER. *(Helps him to his feet.)* All right, come on…easy does it…

SOLOMON. *(As he goes into the bedroom with Walter.)* I'm all right, don't worry—you're very nice people…

> *They exit into the bedroom, closing door. Victor glances at the money in his hand.*

ESTHER. Why are you being so apologetic?

VICTOR. About what?

ESTHER. That old man. Was that his first offer?

VICTOR. *(Crossing L. to D. of table, starts to put money under ashtray but instead puts it in pocket.)* Why do you believe Walter? He was obviously pulling a number out of a hat.

ESTHER. *(Crossing L. a few steps.)* Well, I agree with him. Did you try to get him to go higher?

VICTOR. I don't know how to bargain and I'm not going to start now. You know, you take a tone sometimes—like I'm some kind of an incompetent.

ESTHER. I wish you wouldn't be above everything, Victor, we're not twenty years old. We need this money.

> *He is silent.*

You hear me?

VICTOR. I've made a deal, and that's it.

> *She moves restlessly R. to C.*

59

ESTHER. Well, anyway, you'll get the whole amount.—God, he certainly has changed. It's amazing.

VICTOR. *(Without assent.)* Seems so, ya.

ESTHER. *(Wanting him joining her.)* He's so human! And he laughs!

VICTOR. *(Sitting in chair D. R. of table.)* I've seen him laugh.

ESTHER. *(With a grin of trepidation.)* Am I hearing something or is that my imagination?

VICTOR. I want to think about it.

ESTHER. *(Quietly.)* You're not taking his share? *(!)*

VICTOR. I said I would like to think...

> *Assuming he will refuse the share—she really doesn't know what to do or where to move, so she goes for her purse, which is on sofa, with a quick stride.*

Where you going?

ESTHER. *(Crossing back to C.)* I want to know; are you or aren't you taking his share?

VICTOR. *(Rising, crossing R. to her.)* Esther, I've been calling him all week; doesn't even bother to come to the phone, walks in here and smiles and I'm supposed to fall into his arms?—

ESTHER. I don't understand what you think you're upholding!—

VICTOR. Certain things have happened, haven't they?—I can't turn around this fast, kid; he's only been here ten minutes, I've got twenty-eight years to shake off my back... Now sit down, I want you here.

ESTHER. Don't talk to me like that...

> *She remains standing, uncertain of what to do.*

VICTOR. Please. You can wait a few minutes.

> *She crosses R., sits on sofa.*

ESTHER. *(In despair.)* Vic, it's all blowing away.

VICTOR. *(Crossing R. to hassock. To diminish the entire prize.)* Half of eleven hundred dollars is five-fifty, dear.

ESTHER. I'm not talking about money. He's obviously making a gesture, why can't you open yourself a little?

VICTOR. He's only been here ten minutes. Give me a chance.

ESTHER. My mother was right—I can never believe anything I see. But I'm going to. That's all I'm going to do. What I see.

> *Walter enters from the bedroom carrying his topcoat. Victor sits on sofa, U. of Esther.*

VICTOR. How is he?

WALTER. *(Crossing D., putting coat on back of sofa.)* I think he'll be all right. *(Warmly.)* God, what a pirate! He's eighty-nine!

ESTHER. I don't believe it!

VICTOR. He is. He showed me his...

WALTER. *(At L. of sofa. Laughs.)* Oh, he show you that too?

BOTH. *(Smiling.)* Ya, the British Navy.

ESTHER. *He* was in the British Navy?

VICTOR. *(Building on Walter's support.)* He's got a Discharge. He's not altogether phoney.

WALTER. I wouldn't go that far, A guy that age, though, still driving like that... *(As though admitting Victor was not foolish.)* There is something wonderful about it.

VICTOR. *(Understating.)* I think so.

ESTHER. What do you think we ought to do, Walter?

> *Slight pause. Walter is trying to modify what he believes is his overpowering force so as not to appear to be taking over. He is faintly smiling toward Victor.*

WALTER. There is a way to get a good deal more out of it. I suppose you know that, though. *(?)*

VICTOR. Look, I'm not married to this guy—if you want to call another dealer we can compare.

WALTER. You don't have to do that; he's a registered appraiser— *(Pulling hassock U. a few feet, sits on it.)* You see, instead of selling it, you could make it a charitable contribution.

VICTOR. I don't understand.

WALTER. It's perfectly simple. He puts a value on it—let's say twenty-five thousand dollars, and...

ESTHER. *(Fascinated and with a laugh.)* Are you kidding?

WALTER. It's done all the time. It's a dream world but it's legal—he estimates its highest retail value; which could be put at some such figure. Then I donate it to the Salvation Army; I'd have to take ownership, you see; because my tax rate is much higher than yours so it would make more sense if I took the deduction. I pay around fifty percent tax, so if I make a twenty-five thousand dollar contribution I'd be saving around twelve thousand in taxes. Which we could split however you wanted to. Let's say we split it in half, I'd give you six thousand dollars.

    A pause.

It's really the only sensible way to do it, Vic.

    Esther glances at Victor, but he remains silent.

ESTHER. Would it be costing you anything?

WALTER. On the contrary—it's found money to me. *(To Victor.)* I mentioned it to him just now.

VICTOR. *(As though this had been the question.)* What'd he say?

WALTER. It's up to you. We'd pay him an appraisal fee—fifty, sixty bucks.

VICTOR. Is he willing to do that?

WALTER. Well, of course he'd rather buy it outright, but what the hell…

ESTHER. That's not his decision, is it?

VICTOR. *(Rising, crossing L. to table.)* No…it's just that I feel I did come to an agreement with him and I…

WALTER. Personally, I wouldn't let that bother me—he'd be making fifty bucks for filling out a piece of paper.

ESTHER. That's not bad for an afternoon.

VICTOR. I'd like to think about it.

ESTHER. There's not much time, though, if you want to deal with him.

VICTOR. *(Cornered.)* I'd like a few minutes, that's all.

    Walter, rising, puts hassock back, crosses U. a few steps.

WALTER. *(To Esther.)* Sure…let him think it over. *(To Victor.)* It's perfectly legal, if that's what's bothering you; I almost did it with my stuff but I finally decided to keep it. *(Laughs.)* In fact, my own apartment is so loaded up it doesn't look too different from this.

ESTHER. Well, maybe you'll get married again.

WALTER. *(Crossing D. to U. of hassock.)* I doubt that very much, Esther—I often feel I never should have.

ESTHER. *(Scoffing.)* Why!

WALTER. Seriously. I'm in a strange business, you know—there's too much to learn and far too little time to learn it.—I tried awfully hard to kid myself but there's simply no time for people.

> *Victor looks at him.*

Not the way a woman expects, if she's any kind of woman. *(Laughs.)* But I'm doing pretty well alone!

VICTOR. How would I list an amount like that on my income tax?

WALTER. Well…call it a gift.

> *Victor is silent, obviously in conflict; he sees the emotion.*

…Not that it is, but you could list it as such. It's allowed.

VICTOR. —I was just curious how it…

WALTER. Just enter it as a gift. There's no problem.

VICTOR. I see.

> *Crosses U. to L. of phonograph. Walter feels the first sting of a vague resentment and turns his eyes away. Esther raises her eyebrows, staring at the floor. Walter crosses L. to table, lifts the foil off the table—clearly changing the subject.*

WALTER. You still fence?

> *Crosses R. to C. with foil.*

VICTOR. *(Almost gratefully pursuing this diversion.)* No, you got to join a club and all that. And I work weekends often. I just found it here.

WALTER. *(As though to warm the mood, his desperation growing.)* Mother used to love to watch him do this.

ESTHER. *(Surprised, pleased.)* Really?

WALTER. Sure, she used to come to all his matches.

ESTHER. *(To Victor, somehow charmed.)* You never told me that.

WALTER. Of course; she's the one made him take it up. *(Laughs to Victor.)* She thought it was elegant! Especially with those French gauntlets!

VICTOR. Hey, that's right.

WALTER. *(Laughs at the memory.)* He did look pretty good too!—
> *Spreads his jacket away from his chest.*

I've still got the wounds!
> *Victor glances about, trying to recall where the gauntlets might be.*

VICTOR. *(Recalling.)* Say…!
> *Crosses R. above armchair. Going to his bureau, which is U. R.*

I wonder if they're still…

ESTHER. *(To Walter.)* French gauntlets?

WALTER. *(Crossing R. to L. of hassock.)* She brought them from Paris. Gorgeously embroidered. He looked like one of this musketeers.

VICTOR. Here they are!
> *He lifts a pair of emblazoned gauntlets from offstage drawer.*

What do you know!
> *Crosses D.*

ESTHER. *(Reaching her hand out.)* Aren't they beautiful!
> *He hands her one.*

VICTOR. *(Sitting sofa again U. of Esther.)* God, I'd forgotten all about them.

WALTER. Christmas, 1929.

VICTOR. Look at that, they're still soft… *(To Walter—a little shy in asking.)* How do you remember all this stuff?

WALTER. Why not? Don't you?

ESTHER. He doesn't remember your mother very well.

VICTOR. I remember her. *(Looking at the gauntlet.)* It's just her face; somehow I can never see her.

WALTER. *(Warmly.)* That's amazing, Vic. *(To Esther.)* She adored him.

ESTHER. *(Pleased.)* Did she?

WALTER. Victor? If it started to rain she'd run all the way to school with his galoshes. Her Victor—my God! By the time he could light a match he was already Louis Pasteur.

VICTOR. It's odd…like the harp! I can almost hear the music… But I can never see her face. Somehow.

For an instant, silence, as he looks across at the harp.

WALTER. Vic?

Victor turns to him, eyes swollen with such feeling that reconciliation seems possible.

What's the problem?

Solomon enters from the bedroom. He looks quite distressed. He is in his vest, his tie is open. Without coming D…

SOLOMON. Please, Doctor, if you wouldn't mind I would like to…

Breaks off, indicating the bedroom.

WALTER. What is it?

SOLOMON. *(Indicating the bedroom.)* Just for one minute, please.

Solomon glances at Victor and Esther and returns to the bedroom. Walter turns to Victor. A moment. Victor's gaze remains on Walter, who suddenly is embarrassed and oddly anxious. He glances to Esther, as much to turn from Victor as for any other reason…

WALTER. I'll be right back.

He goes rather quickly up and into the bedroom putting foil on U. furniture. A pause. Victor is sitting in silence, unable to face her. She senses his conflicting feelings and speaks with delicacy and pity.

ESTHER. Why can't you take him as he is?

He glances at her.

Well, you can't expect him to go into an apology, Vic—he probably sees it all differently anyway.

He is silent. She comes to him.

I know it's difficult, but he is trying to make a gesture, I think.

VICTOR. I guess he is, yes.

ESTHER. *(With urging, but sincerely.)* You know what would be lovely? If we could take a few weeks and go to like…out-of-the-way places…just to really break it up and see all the things that people do. You've been around such mean, petty people for so long and little ugly tricks. I'm serious—it's not romantic; we're much too suspicious of everything.

VICTOR. *(Staring ahead.)* Strange guy.

ESTHER. Why?

VICTOR. Well, to walk in that way—as though nothing ever happened.

ESTHER. Why not? What can be done about it?

Victor rises, crosses L. to C. Slight pause.

VICTOR. I feel I have to say something.

ESTHER. *(With a slight trepidation, less than she feels.)* What can you say?

VICTOR. …You think I ought to just take the money and shut up, heh?

ESTHER. But what's the point of going backwards?

VICTOR. You seem to have forgotten everything—I don't mean only right now. It gets to sound as though I invented our whole situation.

Now she avoids his eyes.

That's what throws me sometimes—seriously—like when you talk about the pension. It wasn't only the pension we were after.

ESTHER. *(Glancing U.)* Well, why bring that up now?

Victor crosses L. to table.

VICTOR. *(With a self-bracing tension.)* I'm not going to take this money unless I talk to him.

Victor puts his gauntlet on table. Esther rises, crossing L. to C., leaves her gauntlet on sofa.

ESTHER. *(Frightened.)* You can't bear the thought that he's decent.

He looks at her sharply.

That's all it is, dear. I'm sorry, I have to say it.

VICTOR. (Without raising his voice.) I can't bear that he's *decent. (!)*

ESTHER. You throw this away you've got to explain it to me. You can't go on blaming everything on him or the system or God knows what else! You're free and you can't make a move, Victor, and that's what's driving me crazy!

He is silent, staring at her.

(Quietly.) You take this money! Or I'm washed up. If you're stuck it doesn't mean I have to be.

Movement is heard within the bedroom. She straightens and crosses R., sits on sofa. Victor smooths down his hair with a slow, preparatory motion of his hand, like one adjusting himself for combat. Walter enters from the bedroom, smiling, almost shaking his head.

WALTER. (Crossing D. to C., indicating the bedroom.) Boy—we got a tiger here. What is this between you, did you know him before?

VICTOR. No; why?—what'd he say?

WALTER. He's still trying to buy it outright. (Laughs.) He talks like you added five years by calling him up.

VICTOR. (Rebuking Esther too.) Well, what's the difference, I don't mind.

WALTER. (Registering the distant rebuke.) No, that's fine, that's all right.

A slight look at Esther. Slight pause.

We don't understand each other, do we?

VICTOR. (With a certain thrust.) I am a little confused, Walter... yes.

WALTER. Why is that?

Victor doesn't answer at once.

Come on, we'll all be dead soon!

VICTOR. All right, I'll give you one example—when I called you Monday and Tuesday and again this morning...

WALTER. (Recognizing the inconsistency.) I've explained that.

VICTOR. But I don't make phone calls to pass the time; your nurse sounded like I was a pest of some kind...it was humiliating.

WALTER. *(Oddly, he is over-upset at the reflection on himself.)* I'm terribly sorry, she shouldn't have done that.

VICTOR. I know, Walter, but I can't imagine she takes that tone all by herself.

WALTER. *(Aware now of the depth of resentment in Victor.)* Oh, no—she's often that way. I've never referred to you like that.

    Victor is silent, not convinced.

Believe me, will you? I'm terribly sorry. I'm overwhelmed with work, that's all it is…

VICTOR. *(Crossing R., sits sofa, U. of Esther.)* Well, you asked me, so I'm telling you.

WALTER. Yes! You should! But don't misinterpret that.

    Slight pause. His tension has increased. Crossing R., pulls hassock U. a few feet, sits.

Now about this tax thing. He'd be willing to make the appraisal twenty-five thousand. *(With difficulty.)* If you'd like, I'd be perfectly willing for you to have the whole amount I'd be saving.

    Slight pause.

ESTHER. Twelve thousand?

WALTER. Whatever it comes to.

    Pause. Esther slowly looks to Victor.

You must be near retirement now, aren't you?

ESTHER. *(Excitedly.)* He's past it. But he's trying to decide what to do.

WALTER. Oh. *(To Victor—near open embarrassment now at the atmosphere of rejection.)* It would come in handy, then, wouldn't it?

    Victor glances at him as a substitute for a reply.

I don't need it, that's all, Vic… Actually, I've been about to call you for quite some time now.

VICTOR. What for?

    Suddenly, with a strange quick laugh, Walter reaches and touches Victor's knee.

WALTER. Don't be suspicious!

VICTOR. *(Grinning.)* I'm just trying to figure it out, Walter.

WALTER. Yes, good. All right.

Slight pause.

I thought it was time we got to know one another. That's all.

VICTOR. You know, Walter, I tried to call you a couple of times before this about the furniture—must be three years ago…

WALTER. *(With some tension in his smile.)* I was sick.

VICTOR. *(Surprised.)* Oh… Because I left a lot of messages…

WALTER. I was quite sick. I was hospitalized.

ESTHER. What happened?

Slight pause.

WALTER. *(As though he were not quite sure where he is being led.)* I broke down.

Slight pause.

VICTOR. *(Disarmed.)* I had no idea.

WALTER. Actually, I'm only beginning to catch up with things. I was out of commission for nearly three years. *(With a thrust of success.)* But I'm almost thankful for it now—I've never been happier!

ESTHER. You seem altogether different!

WALTER. I think I am, Esther—I live differently, I think differently. All I have now is a small apartment; and I got rid of the nursing homes…

VICTOR. What nursing homes?

WALTER. *(Attempting a removed self-amusement.)* Oh, I owned three nursing homes; there's big money in the aged, you know—helpless, desperate children trying to dump their parents—nothing like it. I even pulled out of the market. Fifty percent of my time now is in city hospitals. And I tell you, I'm alive. For the first time. I do medicine, and that's it. *(Attempting an intimate grin.)* Not that I don't soak the rich occasionally, but only enough to live, really.

He waits for Victor's comment.

VICTOR. *(With some irony.)* Well, that must be great.

WALTER. *(Seizing on this minute encouragement.)* Vic, I wish we could talk for weeks, there's so much I want to tell you…

It is not unfolding in quite the way he would wish and he must pick examples of his new feelings out of the air.

I never had friends—you probably know that; but I do now. I have good friends.

He rises, crosses L. to L. C., his anxiety rising.

You see… The damned thing happens so gradually. You start out wanting to be the best, and there's no question that you do need a certain fanaticism; there's so much to know and so little time. Until you've eliminated everything extraneous—including people. And of course the time comes when you realize that you haven't merely been specializing in something—something has been specializing in you. You find you've become a kind of instrument, an instrument that cuts money out of people. And it finally makes you stupid; power can do that. You get to think that because you can frighten people they love you. Even that you love them.—And the whole thing comes down to fear. One night I found myself in the middle of my living room, dead drunk with a knife in my hand, getting ready to kill my wife.

ESTHER. Good Lord!

WALTER. Oh ya—and I nearly made it too!

Laughs nervously, crossing R. to hassock.

But there's one virtue in going nuts—provided you survive, of course. You get to see the terror—not the screaming kind, but the slow, daily fear you call ambition, and cautiousness, and piling up the money. *(Sitting hassock.)* And really, what I wanted to tell you for some time now—is that you helped me to understand that in myself.

VICTOR. Me?

WALTER. Yes.

Grins warmly, embarrassed.

Because of what you did. I could never understand it, Vic—after all, you were the better student. And to stay with a job like that through all those years seemed…

He breaks off momentarily with the uncertainty of Victor's reception.

You see, it never dawned on me until I got sick—that you'd made a choice.

VICTOR. A choice, how?

WALTER. You wanted a real life.—And that's an expensive thing; it costs.

> *He senses that perhaps he has found his theme now; he sees he has at last touched something in Victor.*

I'll be frank with you, Vic—I didn't answer your calls this week because I was afraid —I've struggled so long for a concept of myself and I'm not sure I can make it believable to you. But I'd like to.

> *He sees his permission to go on in Victor's perplexed eyes. But it is more difficult too.*

(Rising.) You see, I got to a certain point where…I dreaded my own work; I finally couldn't cut. *(Crossing L. to L. C.)* There are times, as you know, when if you leave someone alone he might live a year or two; while if you go in you might kill him. And the decision is often…not quite, but almost…arbitrary. But the odds are acceptable, provided you think the right thoughts. Or don't think at all, which I managed to do till then.

> *Slight pause.*

I ran into a cluster of misjudgments. It can happen, but it never had to me. There were three cases which had been diagnosed by other men as inoperable. I lost the three. And quite suddenly the…the whole prospect of my own motives opened up. Why had I taken risks that very competent men had declined? And the quick answer, of course, is—to pull off the impossible. Shame the competition.

> *Slight pause.*

(Crossing R. to D. L. of armchair.) But suddenly I saw something else. And it was terror. In dead center, controlling my brains, my hands, my ambition—for thirty years.

> *Slight pause.*

VICTOR. Terror of what?

> *A pause. His gaze is direct on Victor now.*

WALTER. Of it ever happening to me…

> *He glances at the C. chair.*

As it happened to him. Overnight for no reason, to find yourself degraded and thrown-down. *(With the faintest hint of impatience and a challenge.)* You know what I'm talking about, don't you?

> *Victor turns away slightly, refusing commitment. Walter crosses R. to D. of hassock.*

We were both running from the same thing, Vic. I thought I wanted to be tops, but what it was was untouchable:—I ended in a swamp of success and bankbooks, you on Civil Service. The difference is that you haven't hurt other people to defend yourself. And I've learned to respect that, Vic; you simply tried to make yourself useful.

ESTHER. That's wonderful, Walter, to come to such an understanding with yourself.

WALTER. Esther, it's a strange thing; in the hospital, for the first time since we were boys, I began to feel...like a brother. In the sense that we shared something. *(To Victor.)* —And I feel I would know how to be friends now.

> *Victor rises, crossing L. to C. Slight pause. He is unsure.*

VICTOR. Well, fine. I'm glad of that.

> *Walter sees the reserve and presses on more urgently.*

WALTER. You see, that's why you're still so married. That's a very rare thing. And why your boy's in such good shape.—You've lived a real life. *(To Esther.)* But you know that better than I.

ESTHER. *(Hesitates—then emphatically.)* Sometimes. I don't know what I know, Walter.

WALTER. Don't doubt it, dear—believe me, you're fortunate people. *(To Victor.)* You know that, don't you?

VICTOR. *(Looking at Esther.)* I think so.

> *He moves away L. to table.*

ESTHER. It's not quite as easy as you make it, Walter.

> *Walter hesitates, then throws himself into it.*

WALTER. Look, I've had a wild idea—it'll probably seem absurd to you, but I wish you'd think about it before you dismiss it. I gather you haven't decided what to do with yourself now? You're retiring...?

VICTOR. I'll decide one of these days, I'm still thinking.

WALTER. Could I suggest something?

VICTOR. Sure, go ahead.

WALTER. We've been interviewing people for the new wing. For the Administrative side. Kind of liaison people between the scientists and the board. And it occurred to me several times that you might fit in there.

ESTHER. *(With a release of expectation.)* That would be wonderful!

> *Slight pause. Victor glances at her with suppression, but his voice betrays excitement.*

VICTOR. What could I do there though?

WALTER. *(Hopefully, sensing Victor's interest.)* It's kind of fluid at the moment, but there's a place for people with a certain amount of science who…

VICTOR. *(Crossing R. to Walter.)* I have no degree.

WALTER. But you've had analytic chemistry, and a lot of math and physics, if I recall. If you thought you needed it you could take some courses in the evenings.—I think you have enough background.—How would you feel about that?

VICTOR. *(Digging in against the temptation.)* Well…I'd like to know more about it, sure.

ESTHER. *(As though to press him to accept.)* It'd be great if he could work in science, it's really the only thing he ever wanted.

WALTER. I know; it's a pity he never went on with it.

> *Victor crosses L. to table.*

(Turning to Victor.) It'd be perfectly simple, Vic, I'm chairman of the committee. I could set it all up…

> *Victor starts to say something to Walter. Solomon enters. They turn to him surprised.*

SOLOMON. *(Crossing D. to U. L. of sofa.)* Excuse me, go right ahead.

> *Esther sits sofa. Victor sits chair D. R. of table.*

I'm sorry to disturb you. About the harp. If you'll make me a straight out-and-out sale, I would be willing to go another fifty dollars.

WALTER. *(At C.)* Well, you're getting warmer.

SOLOMON. I'm a fair person!—so you don't have to bother with the appraisal and deductions, all right?— *(Before Walter can answer.)* But don't rush, I'll wait. I'm at your service.

> *He goes quickly and worriedly into the bedroom.*

ESTHER. *(Starting to laugh—to Victor.)* Where did you *find* him?

WALTER. That wonderful?—he "made it all ethical"!

> *Esther bursts out laughing, and Walter with her. And as it begins to subside, Walter turns to Victor.*

What do you say, Vic? Will you come by?

> *The laughter is gone. He looks at nothing, as though deciding. The pause lengthens, and lengthens still. Now it begins to seem he may not speak at all. No one knows how to break into his puzzling silence. At last he turns to Walter with a rather quick movement of his head as though he had made up his mind to take the step.*

VICTOR. I'm not sure I know what you want, Walter.

> *Walter looks shocked, astonished, almost unbelieving. But Victor's gaze is steady on him. Walter utters a soundless laugh of incredulity and looks at the floor.*

ESTHER. *(Rising; with a tone of the conciliator shrouding her shock and protest.)* I don't think that's being very fair, is it?

VICTOR. Why is it unfair? We're talking about some pretty big steps here… *(To Walter.)* Not that I don't appreciate it, Walter, but certain things have happened, haven't they? *(With a half-laugh.)* It just seems odd to suddenly be talking about…

WALTER. *(Crossing L. to Victor, downing his resentment.)* I'd hoped we could take one step at a time, that's all. It's very complicated between us, I think, and it seemed to me we might just try to…

VICTOR. *(Rising to R. of chair.)* I know, but you can understand it would be a little confusing.

WALTER. *(Unwillingly, anger peaks his voice.)* What do you find confusing?

> *He considers for a moment, but he cannot go back.*

VICTOR. You must have some idea, don't you?

WALTER. This is a little astonishing, Victor—after all these years you can't expect to settle everything in one conversation, can you?

Victor crosses U. to L. of phonograph.

I simply felt that with a little good will we…we…

He sees Victor's adamant poise.

Oh, the hell with it.

He goes abruptly and snatches a gown and his coat from sofa.

Get what you can from the old man, I don't want any of it.

He goes and extends his hand to Esther, forcing a smile.

I'm sorry, Esther. It was nice seeing you anyway.

Sickened, she accepts his hand. He goes L. toward door.

Maybe I'll see you again, Vic. Good luck.

There are tears in his eyes.

ESTHER. *(Before she can think.)* Walter?

Walter halts at door and turns to her questioningly. She looks to Victor helplessly. But he cannot think either.

WALTER. I don't accept this resentment, Victor. It simply baffles me. I don't understand it. I just want you to know how I feel.

ESTHER. *(Assuaging.)* It's not resentment, Walter.

VICTOR. *(Crossing R. to her, moving hassock D. again.)* The whole thing is a little fantastic to me, that's all. I haven't cracked a book in twenty-five years, how do I walk into a research laboratory?

ESTHER. But Walter feels that you have enough background…

VICTOR. *(Almost laughing over his quite concealed anger at her.)* I know less chemistry than most high school kids, Esther… *(To Walter.)* and physics, yet! Good God, Walter… *(Laughs.)* where you been?

WALTER. I'm sure you could make a place for yourself…

VICTOR. What place? Running papers from one office to another?

WALTER. You're not serious.

Esther sits sofa.

VICTOR. Why? Sooner or later my being your brother is not going to mean very much, is it? I've been walking a beat for twenty-eight years, I'm not qualified for anything technical; what's this all about?

WALTER. *(Putting coat and dress on table.)* Why do you keep asking what it's about? I've been perfectly open with you, Victor!

VICTOR. I don't think you have.

WALTER. *(Crossing R. to D. L. of armchair.)* Why! What do you think I'm...?

VICTOR. *(Crossing L. to D. R. of armchair.)* Well, when you say what you said a few minutes ago, I...

WALTER. What did I say?!

VICTOR. *(With a resolutely cool smile.)* ...What a pity it was that I didn't go on with science?

WALTER. *(Puzzled.)* What's wrong with that?

VICTOR. Oh, Walter, come on, now!

WALTER. But I feel that—I've always felt that.

VICTOR. *(Pointing at the C. chair, a new reverberation sounds in his voice.)* There used to be a man in that chair, staring into space. Don't you remember that?

WALTER. Very well, yes—I sent him money every month.

VICTOR. You sent him five dollars every month.

WALTER. I could afford five dollars. But what's that got to do with you?

VICTOR. What it's got to do with me!

WALTER. Yes, I don't see that.

VICTOR. Where did you imagine the rest of his living was coming from?

WALTER. Victor, that was your decision, not mine.

VICTOR. My decision!

WALTER. We had a long talk in this room once, Victor.

VICTOR. *(Not recalling.)* What talk?

WALTER. *(Astonished.)* Victor! We came to a complete under-standing—just after you moved up here with Dad. I told you then that I was going to finish my schooling come hell or high water, and I advised you to do the same. In fact, I warned you not to allow him to strangle your life. *(To Esther.)* And if I'm not mistaken I told you the same at your wedding, Esther.

VICTOR. *(With an ironic laugh.)* Who the hell was supposed to keep him alive, Walter!

WALTER. *(With a strange fear, more than anger.)* Why did anybody have to? He wasn't sick. He was perfectly fit to go to work.

VICTOR. Work? In 1936? With no skill, no money…?

WALTER. *(Outburst.)* Then he could have gone on welfare! Who was he, some exiled royalty? What did a hundred and fifty million other people do in 1936? He'd have survived, Victor—good God, you must know that by now, don't you?!

> *Slight pause. Suddenly at the edge of fury, and caught by Walter's voicing his own opinion, Victor turns to Esther.*

VICTOR. I've had enough of this, Esther; it's the same old thing all over again, let's get out of here.

> *He starts rapidly U. toward the bedroom.*

WALTER. *(Crossing R. Quickly.)* Vic! Please!

> *He catches Victor, who frees his arm.*

I'm not running him down; I loved him in many ways…

ESTHER. *(Rising; as though conceding her earlier position.)* Vic, listen—maybe you ought to talk about it.

VICTOR. It's all pointless! The whole thing doesn't matter to me!

> *He turns to go to the bedroom.*

WALTER. He exploited you!

> *Victor halts, turns to him, his anger full in his face.*

Doesn't that matter to you?

VICTOR. *(Crossing D. to Walter.)* Let's get one thing straight, Walter—I am nobody's victim.

WALTER. But that's exactly what I've tried to tell you—I'm not trying to condescend.

VICTOR. Of course you are. Would you be saying any of this if I'd made a pile of money somewhere?

> *Walter crosses D. to L. of bench. Dead stop.*

I'm sorry, Walter, I can't take that—I made no choice; the icebox was empty and the man was sitting there with his mouth open.

Slight pause.

I didn't start this, Walter, and the whole thing doesn't interest me, but when you talk about making choices, and I should have gone on with science, I have to say something—just because you want things a certain way doesn't make them that way.

He has ended at a point distant from Walter. A slight pause.

WALTER. *(With affront mixed into his trepidation.)* All right then… How do you see it?

VICTOR. *(Crossing R. above sofa, then D. behind it.)* Look, you've been sick, Walter, why upset yourself with all this?

WALTER. It's important to me!

Victor crosses D. to D. R. of sofa. Tries to smile—and in a friendly way.

VICTOR. But why?—It's all over the dam.

ESTHER. I think he's come to you in good faith, Victor.

He turns to her angrily, but she braves his look.

I don't see why you can't consider his offer.

VICTOR. I said I would think about it.

ESTHER. *(Restraining a cry.)* You know you're turning it down! *(In a certain fear of him, but persisting.)* I mean what's so dreadful about telling the truth, can it be any worse than this?

VICTOR. What "truth"? What are you…?

Solomon suddenly appears from the bedroom.

SOLOMON. Excuse me.

ESTHER. *(At L. of sofa.)* For God's sake, *now* what!

SOLOMON. *(Crossing D. to C.)* I just didn't want you to think I wouldn't make the appraisal; I will, I'll do it…

ESTHER. *(Pointing to the bedroom.)* Will you please leave us alone!

Walter stays D. R. of table.

SOLOMON. *(Suddenly, his underlying emotion—indicating Victor.)* What do you want from him!—He's a policeman! I'm a dealer, he's a doctor, and he's a policeman, so what's the good you'll tear him to pieces?!

ESTHER. Well, one of us has got to leave this room, Victor.

Victor moves to D. L. of sofa.

SOLOMON. Please, Esther, let me...

Going quickly to Walter.

Doctor, listen to me, take my advice—stop it. What can come of this? ...In the first place, if you take the deduction how do you know in two-three years they wouldn't come back to you, whereby they disallow it? I don't have to tell you—the Federal Government is not reliable.

Victor crosses to D. of sofa.

I understand very well you want to be sweet to him *(To Esther.)* but can be two-three years before you'll know how sweet they're going to allow him. *(To Victor and Walter.)* In other words, what I'm trying to bring out, my boys, is that...

ESTHER. ...You want the furniture.

SOLOMON. *(Shouting at her.)* Esther, if I didn't want it I wouldn't buy it! But what can they settle here? It's still up to the Federal Government, don't you see?—if they can't settle nothing they should stop it right now! *(With a look of warning and alarm in his eyes.)* Now please—do what I tell you! I'm not a fool!

He walks out into the bedroom, shaking. Walter crosses up to L. of phonograph.

WALTER. *(After a moment.)* I guess he's got a point, Vic—why don't you just sell it to him; maybe then we can sit down and talk sometime. *(Glancing at the furniture.)* It isn't really a very conducive atmosphere. *(Crossing D.)* —Can I call you?

VICTOR. Sure.

ESTHER. You're both fantastic.

She tries to laugh.

We're giving this furniture away because nobody's able to say the simplest things. You're incredible, the both of you.

WALTER. *(At U. L. of piano bench. A little shamed.)* It isn't that easy, Esther...

ESTHER. Oh, what the hell—I'll say it. *(Crossing L. to C.)* When he went to you, Walter, for the five hundred he needed to get his degree...

VICTOR. *(Crossing to D. L. of sofa.)* Esther! There's no...

ESTHER. It's one of the things standing between you, isn't it?!—Maybe Walter can clear it up. I mean... Good God, is there never to be an end? *(To Walter, without pause.)* Because it stunned him, Walter; he'll never say it, but—

> *She takes the plunge.*

He hadn't the slightest doubt you'd lend it to him. So when you turned him down...

VICTOR. Esther, he was just starting out...

ESTHER. *(In effect, taking her separate road.)* Not the way you told me! Please let me finish! *(To Walter.)* You already had the house in Rye, you were perfectly well established, weren't you?

VICTOR. So what? He didn't feel he could...

WALTER. *(With a certain dread, quietly.)* No, no, I...I could have spared the money... We've never talked about this. I think perhaps we have to.

> *Slight pause.*

(Toward Esther.) It was despicable; but I don't think I can leave it quite that way.

> *Crosses R. to D. L. of hassock. Slight pause.*

Two or three days afterwards... *(To Victor.)* After you came to see me, I phoned to offer you the money.

> *Slight pause.*

VICTOR. Where'd you phone?

WALTER. Here. I spoke to Dad.

> *Esther crosses D., sits piano bench. Slight pause.*

I saw that I'd acted badly, and I...

VICTOR. You didn't act badly...

WALTER. *(With a sudden flight of his voice.)* It was frightful!

> *He gathers himself against his past.*

—We'll have another talk, won't we? I wasn't prepared to go into all this…

Victor is expressionless.

In any case…when I called here he told me you'd joined the Force. And I said—he mustn't permit you to do a thing like that; I said—you had a fine mind and with a little luck you could amount to something in science. That it was a terrible waste. Etcetera. And his answer was—"Victor wants to help me. I can't stop him."

Pause.

VICTOR. You told him you were ready to give me the money?

WALTER. Victor, you remember the…the helplessness in his voice. At that time? With Mother recently gone and everything shot out from under him…?

VICTOR. *(Persisting.)* Let me understand that, Walter; did you tell…?

WALTER. *(In anguish, but hewing to himself.)* There are conversations, aren't there, and looking back it's impossible to explain why you said or didn't say certain things?—I'm not defending it, but I would like to be understood if that's possible.—You all seemed to need each other more, Vic—more than I needed them. To the point where I used to blame myself for a lack of feeling. You understand?—So when he said that you wanted to help him, I felt somehow that it'd be wrong for me to try to break it up between you. It seemed like interfering.

VICTOR. I see… Because he never mentioned you'd offered the money.

WALTER. All I'm trying to convey is that…I was never indifferent; that's the whole point. I did call here to offer the loan—but he made it impossible, don't you see?

VICTOR. I understand.

WALTER. *(Eagerly.)* Do you?

VICTOR. Yes.

WALTER. *(Sensing the unsaid.)* Please say what you think. It's absurd to go on this way. What do you want to say?

Slight pause.

VICTOR. I think it was all…very convenient for you.

WALTER. *(Appalled.)* That's all. *(?)*

> *Walter crosses R. below hassock to sofa.*

VICTOR. *(Crossing L. above hassock to armchair.)* I think so. If you thought Dad meant so much to me—and I guess he did in a certain way—why would five hundred bucks break us apart? I'd have gone on supporting him; it would have let me finish school, that's all.—It doesn't make any sense, Walter.

WALTER. *(With a hint of the hysterical in his tone.)* What makes sense?

VICTOR. You didn't give me the money because you didn't want to.

WALTER. *(Hurt and quietly enraged—slight pause.)* It's that simple. *(?)*

VICTOR. That's what it comes to, doesn't it? Not that you had any obligation, but if you want to help somebody you do it, if you don't you don't.

> *Esther rises, crosses U. a few steps. Victor sees Walter's growing frustration, and Esther's impatience.*

Well why is that so astonishing? We do what we want to do, don't we?

> *Walter doesn't reply. Victor's anxiety rises.*

I don't understand what you're bringing this all up for.

WALTER. You don't feel the need to heal anything. *(?)*

VICTOR. I wouldn't mind that, but how does this heal anything?

ESTHER. *(Crossing to L. of Victor.)* I think he's been perfectly clear, Victor—he's asking your friendship.

VICTOR. By offering me a job and twelve thousand dollars?

> *Esther crosses L. to table.*

WALTER. Why not? What else can I offer you?

VICTOR. But why do you have to offer me anything?

> *Walter is silent, crosses U. few steps, morally checked.*

It sounds like I have to be saved, or something.

WALTER. I simply felt that there was work you could do that you'd enjoy and I…

VICTOR. Walter, I haven't got the education, what are you talking about?

> *Walter crosses D. below sofa then U. and D. behind it.*

You can't walk in with one splash and wash out twenty-eight years. There's a price people pay. I've paid it, it's all gone, I haven't got it anymore. Just like you paid, didn't you?—you've got no wife, you've lost your family, you're rattling around all over the place?—can you go home and start all over again from scratch? This is where we are; now, right here, now. *(Crossing to D. L. of sofa.)* And as long as we're talking, I have to tell you that this is not what you say in front of a man's wife.

WALTER. *(At D. of sofa. glancing at Esther, certainty shattered.)* What have I said…?

VICTOR. We don't need to be saved, Walter!

> *Crosses L. to C. toward Esther.*

I've done a job that has to be done and I think I've done it straight.

> *Turns to Walter.*

You talk about changing your attitudes—well Jesus, kid, I can't see what the hell is changed.

ESTHER. *(Crossing R.)* I want to go, Victor.

VICTOR. *(Stops her at C.)* Please, Esther, he's said certain things and I don't think I can leave it this way.

ESTHER. *(Angrily.)* Well, what's the difference?!

VICTOR. *(Suppressing an outburst.)* Because for some reason you don't understand *anything* anymore!

> *Esther crosses up to D. of armchair. He is trembling as he turns to Walter.*

What are you trying to tell me—that it was all unnecessary? Is that it?

> *Walter is silent.*

Well, correct me, is that the message? Because that's all I get out of this.

WALTER. *(Crossing L. toward Esther.)* I guess it's impossible…

VICTOR. *(The more strongly because Walter seems about to be allied with Esther.)* What's impossible? …What do you *want*, Walter!

WALTER. *(Turning L. of bench.)* I wanted to be of some use. I've learned some painful things, but it isn't enough to know; I wanted to act on what I know.

VICTOR. Act—in what way?

WALTER. *(Knowing it may be a red flag, but his honor is up.)* I feel…
I could be of help. Why live, only to repeat the same mistakes again
and again? I didn't want to let the chance go by, as I let it go before.

    Victor is unconvinced.

And I must say, if this is as far as you can go with me, then you're
only defeating yourself.

VICTOR. *(At D. L. of hassock.)* Like I did before. *(?)*

    Walter is silent.

Is that what you mean?

WALTER. *(Hesitates, then with frightened but desperate acceptance
of combat.)* …All right, yes; that's what I meant.

VICTOR. Well, that's what I thought.—See, there's one thing about
the cops—you get to learn how to listen to people, because if you
don't hear right sometimes you end up with a knife in your back. In
other words, I dreamed up the whole problem. *(?)*

WALTER. *(Casting aside his caution, his character at issue.)* Victor,
my five hundred dollars was not what kept you from your degree!
You could have left Pop and gone right on—he was perfectly fit.

    Victor crosses L. to R. of bench. Esther moves to D. R. of
    armchair.

VICTOR. And twelve million unemployed, what was that, my
neurosis? I hypnotized myself every night to scrounge the outer
leaves of lettuce from the Greek restaurant on the corner? The good
parts we cut out of rotten grapefruit…?

WALTER. I'm not trying to deny…

VICTOR. We were eating garbage here, buster!

    Walter crosses L. to D. R. of table.

ESTHER. But what is the point of…

VICTOR. *(Crossing up to D. L. of armchair. To Esther.)* What are you
trying to do, turn this all into a dream? *(To Walter.)* And perfectly
fit!—What about the inside of his head? The man was ashamed to go
into the street!

ESTHER. But, Victor, he's gone now.

VICTOR. *(With a cry—he senses the weakness of his position.)* Don't tell me he's gone now!—

He is wracked, terribly alone before her.

He was here then, wasn't he? And a system broke down, did I invent that?

ESTHER. No, dear, but it's all different now.

VICTOR. What's different now? Take a walk in the street with your eyes open, kid—we're a goddamned army holding this city down, what do you mean it's different? I'm sorry; I'm on the sidewalk all day, I don't have time to read propaganda.—When it blows again you'll be thankful for a roof over your head!

Crosses D. to R. of Walter.

How can you say that to me? I could have left him with your five dollars a month? I'm sorry, you can't brainwash me—if you got a hook in your mouth don't try to stick it into mine. You want to make up for things, you don't come around to make fools out of people— I didn't invent my life. Not altogether. You had a responsibility here and you walked on it… You can go. I'll send you your half.

He crosses to the harp. Long pause.

WALTER. If you could reach beyond your anger, I'd like to tell you something—Vic.—I know I should have said this many years ago. But I did try… When you came to me I told you…remember I said, "Ask Dad for money." I did say that… He had money left, after the crash.

VICTOR. *(At D. of sofa.)* What are you talking about?

WALTER. He had nearly four thousand dollars.

ESTHER. *(Crossing L. to D. L. of records.)* When?

WALTER. When they were eating garbage here.

Slight pause.

VICTOR. How did you know that?

WALTER. He'd asked me to invest it for him.

VICTOR. Invest it.

WALTER. *(Crossing R. to D. L. of hassock.)* Yes. Not long before he sent you to me for the loan. That's why I never sent him more than

I did. And if I'd had the strength of my convictions I wouldn't have sent him that!

> *There is a pause. Shame is flooding into Victor. He looks at nobody.*

VICTOR. He actually had it?—in the bank?

WALTER. Vic, that's what he was living on, basically till he died. What we gave him wasn't enough; you know that.

VICTOR. But he had those jobs...

WALTER. Meant very little.—He lived on his money, believe me.

> *Victor crosses above Walter to armchair. Walter crosses below hassock to R. of it.*

—I told him at the time, if he would send you through I'd contribute properly. But here he's got you running from job to job to feed him—I'm damned if I'd sacrifice when he was holding out on you. You can understand that, can't you?

> *Victor at the C. chair and shaking his head exhales a blow of anger and astonishment and crosses slowly D. L. Walter crosses L. to C.*

Kid, there's no point getting angry now—you know how terrified he was that he'd never earn anything anymore. And there was just no reassuring him.

VICTOR. *(At D. R. of table. With protest; it is still nearly incredible.)* But he saw I was supporting him, didn't he?

WALTER. For how long, though?

VICTOR. *(Angering.)* What do you mean...how long? He could see I wasn't walking out—

WALTER. I know, but he was sure you would sooner or later.

ESTHER. He was waiting for him to walk out. *(?)*

> *Fearing to inflame Victor, Walter undercuts the obvious answer.*

WALTER. Well...you could say that, yes.

> *Victor sits chair D. R. of table.*

ESTHER. *(Crossing to U. R. of Victor.)* I knew it! God, when do I believe what I see!

WALTER. *(Crossing L. to R. of bench.)* He was terrified, dear... I don't mean he wasn't grateful to you, Vic. He was. But he really couldn't understand it. I may as well say it, Vic—I myself never imagined you'd go that far.

Victor looks at him. Walter speaks with delicacy in the face of a possible explosion.

Well, you must certainly see now how extreme a thing it was, to stick with him like that? And at such cost to you?

Victor is silent.

ESTHER. *(With sorrow.)* He sees it. *(Crossing R. to D. of armchair.)*

WALTER. *(Crossing L. to R. of Victor.)* ...I know we could work together and I'd love to try. What do you say?

Pause.

VICTOR. ...Why didn't you tell me he had that kind of money?

WALTER. But I did when you came to me for the loan.

VICTOR. To "ask Dad"?

WALTER. Yes!

VICTOR. *(Rising.)* But would I have come to you if I had the faintest idea he had four thousand dollars under his ass? It was meaningless to say that to me.

WALTER. Now just a second...

He starts to indicate the harp.

VICTOR. Cut it out, Walter!—I'm sorry, but it's kind of insulting— I'm not five years old! *(Crossing R. below to D. L. of hassock.)* What am I supposed to make of this? You knew he had that kind of money, and came here many times, you sat here, the two of you, watching me walking around in this suit and said nothing? And now you expect me to...?

WALTER. *(Sharply.)* You certainly knew he had *something*, Victor!

VICTOR. What do you want here? What do you want here!

WALTER. *(Crossing R. to Victor.)* Well, all I can tell you is that I wouldn't sit around eating garbage with *that* staring me in the face!

He points at the harp.

Even then it was worth a couple of hundred, maybe more!—Your degree was right there. Right there, if nothing else.

Victor is silent, trembling.

But if you want to go on with this fantasy, it's all right with me. God knows, I've had a few of my own...

He starts for his coat.

VICTOR. Fantasy.

WALTER. *(Turns R. of table.)* It's a fantasy, Victor—your father was penniless and your brother a son of a bitch, and you play no part at all. I said to ask him because you could see in front of your face that he had some money. You knew it then and you certainly know it now.

VICTOR. You mean if he had a few dollars left, that...?

ESTHER. *(Crossing slowly to L. of Victor.)* What do you mean, a few dollars?

VICTOR. *(At D. of hassock. Trying to retract.)* I didn't know he... had four—

ESTHER. But you knew he had something?

VICTOR. *(Caught, as though in a dream where nothing is explicable.)* ...I didn't say that.

ESTHER. Then what are you saying? I want to understand what you're saying!! You knew he had money left?

VICTOR. Not four thousand dol...

ESTHER. But enough to make out?

VICTOR. *(Crying out in anger and for release.)* I couldn't nail him to the wall, could I? He said he had nothing!

ESTHER. But you knew better!?

VICTOR. I don't know what I knew!

> *He has called this out, and his voice and words surprise him. He turns away, cornered by what he senses in himself.*

ESTHER. It's a farce. It's all a goddamned farce!—To stick us into a furnished room so you could send him part of your pay? Even after we were married, to go on sending him money? Put off having children, live like mice—and all the time you knew he...? —Victor, I'm trying to understand you.

VICTOR. *(Turning to her. Roaring out, agonized.)* Stop it!!

> *Esther crosses U. a few steps. Silence. Then...*

I mean, Jesus, you can't leave everything out like this. The man was a beaten dog, ashamed to walk in the street, how do you demand his last buck…?

ESTHER. You're still going to go on saying that?—The man had four thousand dollars!

He is silent.

It was all an act! Beaten dog!—he was a calculating liar! And in your heart you knew it!

He is struck silent by the fact, which is still ungraspable.

(*Crossing to* U. L. *of hassock.*) No wonder you're paralyzed—you haven't believed a word you've said all these years! We've been lying away our existence all these years; down the sewer, day after day after day…to protect a miserable cheap manipulator. No wonder it all seemed like a dream to me—it *was*, a goddamned nightmare. I knew it was all unreal, I knew it and I let it go by.—Well, I can't anymore, kid. I can't watch it another day. *I'm* not ready to die.

She moves toward her purse, crossing above him to sofa, sits on D. *end.*

VICTOR. Esther…

He starts up.

This isn't true either.

ESTHER. We are dying, that's what's true!

VICTOR. (*His voice comes as though from an autonomous part of his body.*) I'll tell you what happened.

She catches the lack of advocacy in his tone, the simplicity. He glances at the C. *chair, then at Walter.*

I did tell him what you'd said to me. I faced him with it.

He doesn't go on, his eyes go to the chair as he crosses up to D. R. *of it.*

Not that I "faced" him, I just told him—"Walter said to ask you."

He stops, his stare is on the C. *chair, caught by memory—in effect, the last line was addressed to the chair.*

WALTER. And what happened?

Pause.

VICTOR. He laughed. And that's when I knew. Because it was that kind of a laugh. But then again it could be a different kind, like a wild joke—because we *were* eating garbage here. *(Crossing D., sitting on hassock.)* And I went out—over to Bryant Park behind the public library.

Slight pause.

The grass was covered with men. Like a big, open-air flop-house. And not bums—some of them still had shined shoes and good hats, busted businessmen, lawyers, skilled mechanics. Which I'd seen a hundred times. But suddenly, you know?—I *saw* it. There was no mercy. Anywhere. *(Glancing at the end chair of the table.)* One day you're the head of the house, at the head of the table, and suddenly you're shit. Overnight. And I tried to figure out that laugh.—How could he be holding out on me when he loved me?

ESTHER. Loved...

VICTOR. *(His voice swelling with sorrow.)* He loved me, Esther! He just didn't want to end up on the grass! It's not that you don't love somebody, it's that you've got to survive. We know what that feels like, don't we?!

She can't answer, feeling the barb.

We do what we have to do, Esther. *(With a wide gesture including her and Walter and himself.)* What else are we talking about here? If he did have something left it was...

ESTHER. "*If*" he had...

VICTOR. *(Rising to L. of hassock.)* What does that change!—I know I'm talking like a fool, but what does that change?—He couldn't believe in anybody anymore, and it was unbearable to me! *(Of Walter.)* He'd kicked him in the face; my mother...

He glances toward Walter as he speaks. There is hardly a pause.

The night he told us he was bankrupt, my mother...

Crosses up to U. L. of sofa.

It was right on this couch.

Walter crosses to L. of phonograph.

She was all dressed up—for some affair, I think. Her hair was piled up, and long earrings? And he had his tuxedo on and made us all sit down; and he told us it was all gone. And she vomited.

Walter, back to audience, bows head. Slight pause.

All over his arms. His hand. Just kept on vomiting, like thirty-five years coming up. And he sat there. Stinking like a sewer.—And a look came onto his face. I'd never seen a man look like that. He was sitting there, letting it dry on his hands.

Pause. He crosses D. to Esther.

What's the difference what you know?

In mourning, Walter crosses slowly D. L. of table to D. of it.

Do you do everything you know?

She avoids his eyes, his charge received.

—Not that I excuse it; it was idiotic, nobody has to tell me that.

Crosses L. toward Walter.

But you're brought up to believe in one another, you're filled full of that crap—you can't help trying to keep it going, that's all. I thought if I stuck with him, if he could see that somebody was still…on his side…

He breaks off, the reason strangely has fallen loose. He crosses, sits bench, facing front.

ESTHER. Yes, I know!

She is close to weeping.

VICTOR. I can't explain it; I wanted to…stop it from falling apart…

He breaks off again. Pause.

WALTER. *(At D. of table. Quietly.)* It won't work, Vic.

Victor looks at him and Esther does.

You see it yourself, don't you?—it's not that at all. You see that, don't you?

VICTOR. *(Quietly, avidly.)* …What.

WALTER. *(Crossing R. to L. of Victor; with a warmth, the heat of his victory.)* Is it really that something fell apart? Were we really brought up to believe in one another? We were brought up to succeed, weren't we? Why else would he respect me so and not you? What fell

91

apart? *(Crossing R. to D. of armchair.)* What was here to fall apart?

Victor looks away at the burgeoning vision.

Was there ever any love here? When he needed her, she vomited. And when you needed him, he laughed. *(Crossing to D. C.)* —What was unbearable is not that it all fell apart, it was that there was never anything here.

Victor turns back to him.

ESTHER. *(As though she herself were somehow moving under the rays of judgment.)* ...But who...can ever face that, Walter?

WALTER. *(To her.)* But you have to! *(To Victor.)* What you saw behind the library that day was not that there was no mercy in the world, kid. It's that there was no love in this house. There was no loyalty.

ESTHER. Except his.

WALTER. Esther, there was nothing here but a straight financial arrangement. That's what was unbearable— *(To Victor.)* And you proceeded to wipe out what you saw.

VICTOR. *(With terrible anxiety.)* Wipe out...

WALTER. Vic, I've been in this box. I wasted thirty years protecting myself from that catastrophe...

Crossing up a few steps. He indicates the chair.

And I only got out alive when I saw that there was no catastrophe, there had never been; they were never lovers—she said a hundred times that her marriage destroyed her musical career. I saw that nothing fell here, Vic—and he doesn't follow me anymore with that vomit on his hands. I don't look high and low for some betrayal anymore; my days belong to me now, I'm not afraid to risk believing someone.—All I ever wanted was simply to do science, but I invented an efficient, disaster-proof, money-maker. You— *(To Esther, with a warm smile.)* You could never stand the sight of blood.

Crosses D. to R. of Victor.

(To Victor.) And what do you do?—march straight into the most violent profession there is. We invent ourselves, Vic, to wipe out what we know. You invent a life of self-sacrifice, a life of duty; but what never existed here cannot be upheld.—You were not upholding something, you were denying what you knew they were. And denying

yourself. *(Crossing l. above bench to l. of Victor.)* And that's all that is standing between us now;—an illusion, Vic. That I kicked them in the face and you must uphold them against me. But I only saw then what you're seeing now; there was nothing here to betray. I am not your enemy. *(Crossing r. to d. l. of hassock.)* It is all an illusion and if you could walk through it, we could meet…

His reconciliation is on him.

…We're brothers. It's almost as though…

He smiles warmly, uncertain still.

…we're like two halves of the same guy.—As though we can't quite move ahead—alone. *(Facing front.)* Do you ever feel that, Vic?

Slight pause.

VICTOR. *(Facing front.)* Walter, I'm trying to trust you. I want to. I…I'll even tell you…there are days when I can't remember what I've got against you. And it hangs in me like a rock. I see myself in a store window, and my hair going, and I'm walking the streets—and I can't remember why. You can go crazy when all the reasons disappear—when you can't even hate anymore.

WALTER. Because it's unreal, Vic, and underneath you know it is.

Slight pause.

VICTOR. Then give me something real.

WALTER. *(Turns to Victor.)* What can I give you?

VICTOR. I'm not blaming you now, I'm asking you. I can understand you walking out. I've wished a thousand times I'd done the same thing. But, to come here through all those years knowing what you knew and saying nothing…

WALTER. *(Agonized, as though unable to deny the past nor to take responsibility for it.)* And if I said… Victor, if I said that I did have some wish to hold you back?—What would that give you now?

Victor rising, turning to Walter. As though he sees the opening toward their old confidence in one another.

VICTOR. Is that what you wanted?—Walter, tell me the truth.

WALTER. *(In a vise.)* I wanted the freedom to do my work. Does that mean I stole your life? *(Crying out.)* You made those choices, Victor! And that's what you have to face!

VICTOR. But what do you face? You're not turning me into a walking fifty-year-old mistake—we have to go home when you leave, we have to look at each other. What do *you* face?

WALTER. I have offered you everything I know how to!

VICTOR. I would know if you'd come to give me something! I would know that!

WALTER. *(Crossing for his coat.)* You don't want the truth, you want a monster!

Esther rises.

VICTOR. *(Following to R. of D. chair.)* You came for the old hand-shake, didn't you! The okay!

Walter halts D. of table.

And you end up with the respect, the career, the money, and the best thing of all, the thing that nobody else can tell you so you can believe it—that you're one hell of a guy and never harmed anybody in your life! Well, you're not going to get it. Not till I get mine.

WALTER. And you? You never had any hatred for me? Never a wish to see me destroyed?

Victor turns away and crosses to D. R. of armchair, Walter follows to D. L. of armchair.

To destroy me, to destroy me with this saintly self-sacrifice, this mockery of sacrifice? What will you give me, Victor!

VICTOR. I don't have it to give you. Not anymore. And you don't have it to give me. And there's nothing to give—I see that now. I just didn't want him to end up on the grass. And he didn't. And that's all it was. I couldn't work with you, Walter. I can't. I don't trust you.

WALTER. Vengeance. Down to the end. He is sacrificing his life to vengeance.

ESTHER. Nothing was sacrificed.

WALTER. To prove with your failure what a treacherous son of a bitch I am—to hang yourself in my doorway. Then and now.

ESTHER. *(Quietly, not facing either of them.)* Leave him, Walter, please. Don't say any more.

WALTER. You quit. Both of you. You lay down and quit, and that's the long and short of all your ideology. It is all envy!—And to this moment you haven't the guts to face it! You are a failure. But your failure does not give you moral authority! Not with me! I worked for what I made—and there are people walking around today who'd have been dead if I hadn't. Yes.

He points at the c. chair.

He was smarter than all of us—he saw what you wanted and he gave it to you! He killed our mother and he killed you. But not me. Not then and not now.

Solomon opens bedroom door, stands in it.

He will never kill me.

Humiliated by her. He is furious.

(*To Solomon.*) Go ahead, you old mutt—rob them blind, they love it! (*Turns to Victor.*) You will never, never again make me ashamed!

He turns to go. A gown lies on the table beside his coat. Suddenly he sweeps it up and flings it at Victor with an outcry. He picks up his coat from table, exits. Victor exits after him.

VICTOR. Walter! Walter!

SOLOMON. (*Crossing d. to c.*) Let him go. (*Calling to Victor who is off L.*) What can you do?

Victor enters, crosses R., puts dress on table, stands d. of table.

ESTHER. Whatever you see, huh. *(?)*

Solomon turns to her, questioningly.

—You believe what you see.

SOLOMON. (*Thinking she was rebuking him.*) What then?

ESTHER. No—it's wonderful. Maybe that's why you're still going. I was nineteen years old when I first walked up those stairs—if that's believable. And he had a brother, who was the cleverest, most wonderful young doctor…in the world. As he'd be soon. Somehow, someway. And a rather sweet, inoffensive gentleman, always waiting for the news to come on… And next week, men we never saw or heard of will come and smash it all apart and take it all away. —Why is finality always so unreal? So many times I thought—the one thing he wanted most was to talk to his brother, and that if they could— But he's come and he's gone. And I still feel it—isn't that terrible? It always seems to me that one little step more—and some crazy kind of forgiveness will come, and lift up everyone. When do you stop being so…foolish?

SOLOMON. I had a daughter, should rest in peace, she took her own life. That's nearly sixty years. And every night I lay down to sleep—she's sitting there. I see her clear like I see you. But if it was a miracle and she came to life—what would I say to her?— *(Crossing L. to Victor, taking money from pocket.)* So come, let's settle it now. *(To Victor, paying out.)* So you got there seven; so I'm giving you eight, nine, ten, eleven…

> *Searches, finds a fifty.*

And there's a fifty for the harp. Now you'll excuse me—I got a lot of work here tonight.

> *Solomon gets his pad and pencil, and begins carefully listing each piece, as he crosses and sits in armchair. Victor folds the money, puts it in pocket as he crosses R. to Esther.*

VICTOR. We could still make the picture, if you like.

ESTHER. Okay.

> *He goes to his suit on sofa and begins to rip the plastic wrapper off, as he crosses toward U. L.*

Don't bother.

> *He turns at U. R. of table, looks at her. She picks up her purse from sofa and crosses L. to Solomon.*

Goodbye, Mister Solomon.

> *Solomon looks up from his pad. They shake hands.*

SOLOMON. Goodbye, dear—I like that suit, that's very nice.

> *He returns to his work.*

ESTHER. Thank you.

> *She walks to door with her life. Victor puts on his holster, pulls up his tie.*

VICTOR. When will you be taking it away?

SOLOMON. With God's help if I'll live—first thing in the morning.

VICTOR. *(Of the suit.)* I'll be back for this later, then. And there's my foil, and the mask, and the gauntlets.

SOLOMON. *(Continuing his work.)* Don't worry, I wouldn't touch it.

Victor picks up cap and crosses R. to Solomon.

VICTOR. *(Extending his hand.)* I'm glad to have met you, Solomon.

SOLOMON. *(Rising, shaking hands.)* Likewise. And I want to thank you.

VICTOR. What for?

SOLOMON. *(With a glance at the furniture.)* Well…who would ever believe I would start such a thing again…?

He cuts himself off.

But go—go, I got a lot of work here.

VICTOR. *(Starting to the door, putting on cap.)* Good luck with it.

SOLOMON. Good luck you can never know till the last minute, my boy.

VICTOR. Right.

Smiles, stops at D. of table, turns to Solomon.

Yes. *(With a last look around at the room.)* Well…bye-bye.

SOLOMON. *(As Victor goes out with Esther.)* Bye-bye, bye-bye.

> *He is alone. He puts the pad and pencil in his pocket. He looks about, and the challenge of it all oppresses him and he is afraid and worried. His hand goes to his cheek, he pulls his flesh in fear. Then his eye falls on the phonograph. He goes to it, inspects it, then looks at the record on the turntable. He switches the turntable on. It is the Laughing Record. He smiles, then chuckles. Now as he sits in the armchair he laughs, the laughter of the record combining with his. He leans back sprawling in the chair, laughing with tears in his eyes, howling helplessly to the air.*

CURTAIN

AUTHOR'S PRODUCTION NOTE

A fine balance of sympathy should be maintained in the playing of the roles of Victor and Walter. The actor playing Walter must not regard his attempts to win back Victor's friendship as mere manipulation. From entrance to exit, Walter is attempting to put into action what he has learned about himself, and sympathy will be evoked for him in proportion to the openness, the depth of need, the intimations of suffering with which the role is played.

This admonition goes beyond the question of theatrics to the theme of the play. As the world now operates, the qualities of both brothers are necessary to it; surely their respective psychologies and moral values conflict at the heart of the social dilemma. The production must therefore withhold judgment in favor of presenting both men in all their humanity and from their own viewpoints. Actually, each has merely proved to the other what the other has known but dared not face. At the end, demanding of one another what was forfeited to time, each is left touching the structure of his life.

The play can be performed with an intermission, as indicated at the end of Act One, if circumstances require it. But an unbroken performance is preferable.

PROPERTY LIST

(Use this space to create props lists for your production)

SOUND EFFECTS

(Use this space to create sound effects lists for your production)